PROVEN STRATEGIES
for
EFFECTIVE COMMUNITY ORIENTED POLICING

Detective Lieutenant
Steven L. Rogers

43-08 162nd Street
Flushing, NY 11358
www.LooseleafLaw.com
800-647-5547

Any resemblance to the names in the scenarios and actual people is pure coincidence, completely unintentional and not the responsibility of the author.

Library of Congress-in-Publication Data

Rogers, Steven L., 1951-
  Proven strategies for effective community oriented policing / Steven L. Rogers.
      p. cm.
  Includes index.
  ISBN 978-1-932777-70-3 (pbk.)
  1. Community policing--United States. I. Title.
  HV7936.C83R644 2008
  363.2'3--dc22
                                        2008042287

Printed in the United States of America

Cover design by *Sans Serif, Inc.* Saline, Michigan

TABLE OF CONTENTS

This Book Is Dedicated to the Members
Of the World's Greatest Peacekeeping Force

American Police Officers

To maintain at all times a relationship with the public that gives reality to the historic tradition that the police are the public and the public are the police: the police being only the members of the public that are paid to give full-time attention to the duties which are incumbent on every citizen in the interest of community welfare and existence.

— SIR ROBERT PEEL
19th Century

i

D et./Lt. Steven Rogers is a thirty-two year veteran of the Nutley, New Jersey Police Department. He is presently Commander of the police department's Criminal Investigation Division and Internal Affairs Bureau.

In 1982, he graduated from William Paterson University with a BS degree in Criminal Justice Administration. He completed several courses on National Military Strategy at the United States Naval War College in 1998 and served as a Lieutenant Commander with the United States Naval Reserve as the United States Northern Command's Senior Intelligence Officer assigned to the FBI Joint Terrorism Task Force, Washington D.C. in 2002.

Presently, he is the Naval Reserve Association's National Vice President for Junior Officers Programs. Det/Lt Rogers is a member of the Nutley NJ Board of Education.

In 1991, as a national speaker and lecturer, was selected by the New Jersey Attorney General to lecture at the Israeli National Police Academy on issues related to community policing.

He frequently appears on nationally syndicated news broadcasts, which include CNN, FOX, and MSNBC, and he is an Honored Lifetime Member of Biltmore Who's Who.

ACKNOWLEDGMENTS

Commission of Accreditation for Law Enforcement Agencies
(CALEA)
Montclair NJ Police Department
Nutley NJ Police Department
Professor James Vivinetto, Caldwell College, Caldwell NJ
ABA Division for Public Education
Columbia South Carolina Police Department
New Haven Connecticut Police Department
Somerville Mass Police Department
Ft Meyers, Florida Police Department
Bridgeport Connecticut Police Department
Federal Bureau of Investigation
Canadian Teachers Federation
Bureau of Justice Statistics, Department of Justice
Star Ledger Newspaper, Newark NJ
Volunteers in Police Service (VIPS)
National Association of Crime Victims Compensation Boards

Special Thanks to: Police Chief Sam Hargadine, Iowa City Police
Department and Public Affairs Officer Bill Rosop, Mount
Prospect, Illinois Police Dept.

Much of the research with regard to surveys and statistics were
obtained from public information sources provided by the
individuals listed above and organizations on the World Wide
Web.

INTRODUCTION

The legitimate object of government is to do for a community of people whatever they need to have done, but cannot at all do in their separate and individual capacities.
— PRESIDENT ABRAHAM LINCOLN

I n order to preserve our precious freedoms we must take responsibility for our own actions and that of our freely elected government. The environment, which we establish as a society, through the decisions each and every citizen makes with regard to public policies, affects business, industry, education, our infrastructure, and the administration of justice. All have a profound impact on the communities in which we live and work. Simply put, we get the type of government by the type of people we elect to office.

From 1776 to the present day, Americans have always made it a point to "get involved" with community-based programs which enhance their quality of life and safety. In the past, many of these programs were integrated into community policing methodologies which created a powerful proactive crime-fighting partnership between the people and the police.

However, during the late 20th Century, many Americans lost their will and desire to commit themselves to community-based programs which historically have strengthened law enforcement efforts to prevent and fight crime because their elected officials did not "walk the talk" and failed to provide leadership, inspiration, and more importantly the funding needed to advance proactive police-community programs designed to prevent crime and enhance the relationship between the police and the people.

Many politicians campaign in neighborhoods throughout the entire nation, promising funding to police departments and community groups striving to implement new and effective crime-fighting techniques via community policing programs. However, these politicians fail to deliver on their promises, resulting in the fragmentation of police-public partnerships, and the creation of widespread public apathy.

It took an act of war on September 11th, 2001, for the American people to once again "get involved" with the police, not just to improve their quality of life and to establish proactive crime-fighting methodologies, but also to become partners in the global war on terrorism which gave birth to a new kind of criminal dedicated to the mission of destroying our nation, city by city and block by block.

Unfortunately, several years after 9/11 when the "support our police" rallying cry of the people was heard in every state, town, and city across the nation, the streets once again became silent as a result of politicians not "walking the talk." They failed to deliver on their promises to fund homeland security projects which are earmarked to be integrated with community-based policing programs. The failure of our political leaders has caused many cities and towns across the nation to slowly slip into very dangerous waters which has the potential to bring chaos to our streets, violence to our schools, and the birth of a soaring crime rate never before witnessed in the history of this nation.

With the threat of a new kind of *criminal warrior* roaming our streets, now more than ever, community policing is perhaps America's best chance to win what might become a fight for national survival.

Police departments in the United States are the most technologically advanced law enforcement organizations in the world. American police departments are well prepared to react effectively to all kinds of criminal activity.

However, the enemies we will be facing in this new century are not the traditional criminal types. Instead, they are criminal warrior types, never before seen on the streets of our nation.

This brand of criminal roaming our streets and plotting to destroy our quality of life isn't satisfied with a break-in, a robbery, or an assault. This criminal warrior is only satisfied with *death and destruction*. He or she enters our neighborhood as a member of a gang, drug cartel, organized crime, or terrorist organization.

Police officers and citizens from every city and town across America are facing their greatest challenges. These challenges will require police administrators to shift priorities from traditional crime fighting methodologies to a new kind of tactical policing which can win the war against criminal elements only with the full cooperation and active participation of the public.

All the high-tech equipment police departments have installed in patrol cars and headquarters buildings throughout our nation are no match for the criminal warriors about to come to the streets of America.

It will be through police—public partnerships designed to enhance intelligence capabilities and information sharing—that will enable us to succeed in defeating the enemies of our society before they defeat us.

Until the American people and the leaders they elect to office are willing to address in a very decisive manner the challenges America's law enforcement community will be facing in the next few years, every citizen in every neighborhood better prepare for the future with an understanding that the worst is yet to come.

It is imperative that all of us awaken to the fact that police-community partnerships dedicated to strengthen law enforcement efforts to prevent and fight crime is our nation's most important crime-fighting tool.

The failure to implement community policing methodologies designed to identify criminal activity, increase intelligence capabilities, and share vital information with other law enforcement agencies, will have profound negative impact on our way of life.

It is an absolute necessity for police executives to convey to every patrol officer that the duties they perform and how they perform them will have profound impact on the security of the neighborhoods they patrol and on the security of our nation.

This book provides citizens, police executives, and patrol officers with historical insight on how police-community relations fragmented in the 20th Century and the importance of restoring that relationship in the fight for America's survival. It also provides the foundational tools necessary to build a positive and productive partnership between the police and the people as we face very serious challenges in the next few years.

Community policing has always been, and is today, America's best chance to win the fight against crime and to win the fight against the new powerful *criminal warrior* plotting to take over our country, neighborhood by neighborhood.

As we enter this new century, with this new challenge, against a new enemy, let us keep in mind the words of President Abraham Lincoln who met the challenges of his time:

The dogmas of the past are inadequate to the stormy present. The occasion is piled high with difficulty, and we must rise with the occasion. As our case is new, we must think anew, and act anew.

Detective Lieutenant Steven L. Rogers

CHAPTER 1
LEADERSHIP

Leadership is intangible, therefore no weapon ever designed can replace it.

— GENERAL OMAR BRADLEY

Leadership in the police profession carries with it responsibilities unlike any other occupational field. The decisions executives, police supervisors, and patrol officers make daily have direct impact on the people who live and work in the community they serve.

On a grander scale, the public policy decisions made by law enforcement officers and administrators directly impact our entire criminal justice system on the local, state, and national level. Every decision a police officer or law enforcement executive makes reflects how government responds to the crime problems we are faced with today.

The most difficult problems law enforcement leaders face each and every day emanates from within the internal structure of the law enforcement organization in which they are employed. Low morale, unproductive officers, apathy, lack of commitment, training shortfalls, and manpower issues, are a few of the many problems which affect the overall capability of the police to meet public safety demands.

For over four decades police executives have debated the various reasons why serious internal organizational problems in police organizations exist. The one common thread which the majority of law enforcement executives always find "pulled" from the "fabric" which keeps the police organization together, is the failure of command level executives and middle level managers to effectively lead.

Police department management failures rests solely on the shoulders of the individuals who occupy the highest ranks in the organization. It is ultimately the command staff's responsibility to place the right people, in the right positions, to do the right job.

1

In a survey conducted by the New Jersey Community Policing Officers' Association in the late 90s, numerous New Jersey police officers of all ranks were asked to rate their law enforcement agency's leadership structure. Over 90% of the officers surveyed stated that they were aware of serious leadership problems in their individual police agencies. Furthermore, they identified upper management's failure to establish a management process and philosophy designed to enhance continuity in decision-making and in enforcing policies which clearly defined the scope and mission of the organization as a major management failure.

This survey also revealed that common leadership failures in the police profession usually result in a fragmented interpretation and execution of policy. For example, many police officers from various police departments which maintain a three-shift schedule will complain that they work for three different police departments, one department for each shift because "the boss on the day shift interprets department policy totally different than the boss on the evening and midnight shifts."

Leadership failures such as a command staff's failure to clearly define goals and objectives result in confusion, lack of direction and differing views on enforcement procedures and police operations. A lack of effective leadership turns what should be a shared vision between police commanders and the rank and file, into a shared nightmare.

Instability in the leadership structure of the police organization results in the fragmentation of the rank and file, deterioration of discipline and order, and eventually a total breakdown in operational effectiveness.

The blame for leadership and mission failure rests solely on what many police officers call "the ivory tower mentality style of leadership."

Police executives and supervisors who live and work in the famed ivory tower rarely know what is happening on the streets or in the neighborhoods of their community. The ivory tower is seen by patrol officers as a wall of separation between the rank and file and management, thus further alienating command and supervisory personnel from the men and women working on the streets.

Patrol officers and detectives justifiably complain that ivory tower leaders rarely, if ever, seek their input, opinions, suggestions, or ideas when specific public safety or quality of life issues need to be addressed by the police department.

Many leaders in the police profession are too comfortable in their ivory tower. They are part of an institutional cancer that hinders progress by refusing to allow fresh innovative ideas to flourish. Hence, the feeling among patrol officers and others is that they are *apart from* instead of *a part of* the agency that employs them.

In past years, ivory tower leaders were tolerated or ignored. They are the "dead weight" which must be removed from the profession before any progress can be made. Since our nation relies on local, state, and federal police departments to protect our society from criminal activity, we can no longer afford to tolerate *ivory tower leadership*; nor can we afford to spend time, manpower, and money listening to their endless arguments against change.

Police leaders sitting in the ivory tower must accept change or be forced to leave office. The public must acknowledge the need to change policing strategies and tactics, or be forced into a kind of change that will be delivered to their neighborhoods by criminal enterprises, gangs, and terrorists.

The Police Sergeant as a Leader

Every young man and woman who enters a police academy graduates as a trained and disciplined professional law enforcement officer. When he/she sees superior officers, they salute. When they speak to their supervisors they reply, "Yes, Sir" and "No, Sir." When in uniform, he/she is well groomed and well-dressed.

Soon after many new recruits leave the academy and join the rank and file of their police department, they inevitably come in contact with the *negatrons*; a group of officers who complain endlessly about their job, their bosses, and just about everything under the sun.

Negatrons have great impact on the efficiency of police departments. These disgruntled cops are very successful in sapping morale, causing dissension, and leading good cops into bad situations.

When the new recruit is exposed to the *club of negatrons*, the transformation from the well-mannered, groomed, and disciplined cop, to the cop who no longer salutes his superior officers or uses as part of his or her vocabulary "Yes, Sir" and "No, Sir," does not take very long.

Police sergeants are usually the supervisors who ignore and tolerate this group of unprofessional officers allowing them to *contaminate* weak-willed police officers who eventually become charter members of the infamous "blue wall of silence club." Once a few dozen officers are contaminated, it doesn't take long for the entire police department to become *infected*. Order, discipline, and morale breaks down and the overall efficiency of the police department will rapidly diminish.

In this 21st Century, police officers in America are going to find themselves engaging not only common criminals, but violent gangs and possibly foreign terrorists.

Unless police sergeants, who are the first-line supervisors in all police departments, rein in the negatrons that are contaminating the rank and file, the *field of battle* will be filled with the blood of men and women wearing blue, instead of with the blood of *criminal warriors* attempting to take over our neighborhoods.

First-line supervisors must demonstrate that they have the courage to correct problems that have the potential of breaking down the operational efficiency of their police department.

Sergeants will have to use leadership skills designed to isolate the negatrons and to persuade good officers to fulfill the vital mission of defending our nation though a shared vision.

The Police Chief / Captain / Lieutenant as Leaders

As a police supervisor and naval officer for nearly thirty-one years, I have always believed that in order to gain the respect of our troops we must constantly project characteristics which portray courage, acceptance of responsibility, self-control, knowledge, politeness, attitude of service, comradeship, modesty, self-respect and high moral standards.

Those of us in upper level and middle management leadership positions need to understand that our subordinates view us from two sets of eyes. The first view is from the physical eye, which sees us on the job performing our sworn duty. The second view is from the "mind's eye," which sees us in our personal lives at home, with the spouse, the children, or amongst the general population. I believe it is the view from the mind's eye that has the most impact on subordinates.

If a subordinate sees his or her leader treating his family and friends with respect, the impact will be positive. If the actions of the leader are less than honorable, the impact on a subordinate could be devastating.

The character of a leader plays an important role in effective leadership. General Lemuel C. Shepherd, Jr, USMC (Ret.) once said:

> *"Character in my opinion is the greatest of man's virtues. It is a distinctive trait that governs an individual's patterns of behavior and is indicative of moral strength."*

Personal example is that character which conveys to each subordinate that they will be expected to do nothing that the leader has not done. If a leader is indecisive, looks shabby and projects an apathetic attitude toward the organization, the troops will lose confidence in him or her, morale will suffer, and someone may lose their life because discipline and order will break down. Leaders should convey to their troops that they (leaders) are in command! Leaders should look sharp, speak clearly, and command attention when they walk into a room.

Character is an important foundation of leadership. Without the characteristics which demonstrate that a leader could take care of himself or herself, there is no way that a leader will be able to convince the officers under his or her command that he or she has the ability to lead.

From early in their career, police officers should begin the process of building the leadership foundations they will stand upon for the rest of their lives.

I have always told police recruits:

> *"Mold yourself into a shining example of a police*
> *officer that people will trust and admire."*

The responsibilities of today's police supervisors are far greater than their predecessors of yesteryear. The conduct of the sergeant, lieutenant, captain and chief, off duty as well as on duty, will in some way impact the lives of the men and women working under their command.

The leadership principles police supervisors should follow are similar to the principles many military leaders follow when leading their troops into peacekeeping or combat missions. These principles promote cohesiveness, teamwork, morale and a shared vision and determination to accomplish the assigned mission.

Individuals in police leadership positions must strive to educate themselves about the local and global perspectives on issues they come directly or indirectly involved with.

Successful police supervisors occupy themselves with matters other than what they hear on the radio, read in newspapers, or watch on television. Effective leaders need more than just "local news" as a learning tool. They need to constantly expand their horizons by gathering information and knowledge that will help them perform their duty effectively. The more knowledge a police supervisor obtains by studying who, what, when, where, why and how of present-day issues, the better prepared he or she will be to address the leadership issues challenging them tomorrow.

Learning is a constant for the effective police leader. Gaining knowledge about the skills and talents of each officer under his or her command and learning about the people who live and work in each neighborhood of the community is an absolute necessity to build successful police community partnerships.

Community Policing & Effective Leadership

One of the first steps in building a successful community policing program is to institutionalize leadership methodologies which can be utilized by every member of the police department from the office of Chief to the patrol officer on the street.

One of the most effective methodologies used by innovative and progressive leaders is known as Management-by-Walking Around (MBWA).

I first learned of this leadership concept from a book I read about Abraham Lincoln. President Lincoln made it a point to visit the field of battle to meet with his troops, asking questions about their morale, the war effort, and their ideas and opinions on how to end the war.

Lincoln was a people president. Many of his decisions were based on what his troops shared with him, not just on what his commanders told him. Lincoln used the MBWA method of leadership to convey to his troops that what they said and how they felt meant very much to him.

Police commanders could also use MBWA as a management tool to learn from the patrol officers working the streets, and the people who live in the neighborhoods of the towns and cities being patrolled.

Everyone in police work is a leader. The command staff of the police force must make it a priority to take care of the patrol officers by staying in touch with them. By employing MBWA, command staff personnel could tap into the thoughts, ideas, opinions, and suggestions of the men and women patrolling the streets. They are in the best position to provide the best ideas to combat crime in the neighborhoods where they work. Also, patrol officers can employ MBWA by tapping into the thoughts, ideas, and suggestions of the people who live and work in the community. Who knows better than the *neighborhood people* as to what is best for their quality of life.

The MBWA leadership methodology strengthens law enforcement core values which could have profound impact on the very survival of the police organization and its overall effectiveness in protecting the public.

With regard to community policing, leadership is an influence process dependent upon the relationship between leaders (police) and followers (citizens). Law enforcement agencies can accomplish very much through a process of people working together with the police to achieve shared goals and aspirations.

Police leaders can use MBWA as a tool to convey a willingness to encourage the people in the community to become *a part of* the law enforcement effort, via community policing programs.

Whether you are a police commander seeking input from the patrol officers on the street, or a patrol officer seeking input from the citizens in the community, there are some effective methods of communication which can be used to make MBWA a worthwhile effort.

Effective Methods of Communication

- Always be in control and project confidence and a positive attitude.

- Listen to what people are saying to you and respond to their input.

- Visit patrol officers and/or neighborhoods spontaneously.

- When chatting with officers or citizens, talk about their needs, wants, and desires.

- Ask for suggestions, ideas, and thoughts on public safety issues, operations, etc.

- Commend the officers who are doing a good job.

- Let citizens know they are a vital part of the law enforcement effort.

- Share the police department vision. Let them know they are a part of it.

Successful police leaders are self-starters, knowledgeable and confident. They know how to infuse important transcending values into an enterprise.

Three Leadership Skills for the Effective Police Supervisor

Communication is an art. Effective police leaders must be skilled mediators, negotiators, and diplomats.

Leaders need to master:

- **THE SKILL TO MOTIVATE:** This is accomplished by sharing the police department's vision and giving officers a sense of ownership.

- **THE SKILL TO EMPOWER:** Delegating authority and decision-making makes officers a part of the law enforcement process.

- **THE SKILL TO TAKE RISKS:** Risk takers are the people who usually succeed.

By employing these skills, police department leaders will see a vast improvement in officer initiated performance; team work; a willingness to embrace change; and building trust among peers and management.

A good police department is led by men and women who listen to the voices of the people who live and work in the neighborhoods, and who listen to the concerns, suggestions, and ideas of the police officers who work in those neighborhoods.

An effective leader understands his subordinates, unites them, directs them toward a common goal, inspires them, motivates them, and gives them a sense of ownership and purpose.

> *"Don't tell people how to do things, tell them what to do and let them surprise you with their results."*
> – GEORGE S. PATTON

He who rejects change is the architect of decay.
— HAROLD WILSON

During the latter part of the 20th Century, police executives nationwide were grappling with the effects of negative publicity the police profession was facing as a result of high profile cases involving officers charged with misconduct, excessive use of force, and corruption.

Police executives concluded that the one common denominator which law enforcement agencies nationwide were suffering from was the lack of positive police-public contact.

America's law enforcement community needed to revisit the positive impact community policing had on police agencies in the 19th Century, and then re-shape this policing methodology to meet 21st Century policing challenges.

In the late 1990s, there was general agreement among law enforcement practitioners that police executives who ignored internal problems which continuously eroded the morale and performance of police personnel allowed their agencies to become ineffective and in some cases an embarrassment to the law enforcement profession.

By the end of 1996, addressing issues related to the image of the police became a top priority in many police departments across America, resulting in aggressive campaigns to change the image of policing by confronting head-on, long-ignored problems related to how police officers interacted with the public.

These campaigns encouraged police departments to change their traditional reactive policing methodologies to comprehensive proactive community policing methodologies which were integrated into the entire law enforcement operations process.

The introduction of community policing not only meant a re-evaluation of how the police interacted with the community, but how the police interacted with the police.

It was the close examination of the police-police relationship which resulted in the quick action of many police executives to clean up their agencies internally, as a precursor to cleaning up the crime problems in neighborhoods they were responsible to protect.

During the 1970s and 1980s, many law enforcement agencies witnessed the emergence of a police subculture, commonly known as the "five percenters." Members of this infamous group are identified as police officers who compromise their oath of office by committing unethical or illegal acts.

Five percenters usually apply peer pressure on good officers and encourage them to become part of what is commonly known as the "blue wall of silence," seeking their "silence" when unethical or illegal activity is being investigated by the police department.

An unfortunate problem many police departments must confront is the fact that far too many police officers choose to become one of the "building blocks" of the blue wall when they witness corruption, brutality, and other unethical or illegal acts committed by other officers.

It has always been a mystery to many police investigators as to why bad cops are protected by good cops in view of the fact that if during an investigation it is found that the good cop witnessed a criminal act and covered it up, he or she would be prosecuted along with the bad cop.

Keeping silent is not an escape from the criminal or unethical act being investigated. It is an invitation to become a part of the act which can result in severe consequences.

Fortunately, in the late 1990s the "blue wall of silence" in hundreds of police departments across America began to crumble as community policing began to impact the way police officers performed their duties and how they interacted with each other.

Community policing brings to surface good cops who are tired of being stigmatized and stereotyped as being bad cops because of the unlawful and reckless behavior of the few cops who compromise their integrity.

One by one, good cops are confronting the five percenter problem by refusing to yield to negative peer pressure and by refusing to become a "block" in the blue wall of silence.

By the late 90s, police departments began to employ better educated police officers who filled the ranks of patrolman to chief. Many of these police officers are fully committed to doing a good job policing their communities and to keep their own neighborhoods, and the police department, honest.

Although the five percenter movement is on the decline, a new sub-culture in the police profession is on the rise. This sub-culture consists of police officers who are identified as the "generation of entitlement."

These officers oppose anything a police executive does to advance the police department's goals and objectives and do not concern themselves with earning respect, good pay, and a good working environment. In their eyes, customs, traditions, and a good work ethic which promotes dedication and commitment are things of the past. They believe they are entitled to these things.

Officers who are identified as members of the generation of entitlement become the *negatrons* of the law enforcement profession. They create an "us against them" attitude and use peer pressure to gain support for their positions which usually oppose management decisions which are designed to have positive impact on police operations.

The "generation of entitlement club" surfaces on two levels in the police chain of command. The first level consists of first-line supervisors – patrol sergeants. These are the supervisors who display apathy, lack of vision, and fail to understand the need for change. Without the support of the first-line supervisors, it is nearly impossible for the upper management of the police command structure to succeed in implementing policy changes.

The second level in the police chain of command where this *club* has influence is with the rank and file – the patrol force. These officers (only a small number) are narrow-minded and live in a fantasy world which portrays police work in a *Hollywood*-type setting. Most of the officers who are members of this *club* lack the much needed education now required to effectively address the quality of life and public safety issues many citizens face today.

Negatrons and members of the generation of entitlement club are the architects of decay in the police profession.

It is imperative that police executives decisively address the negative impact these officers have on their entire agency before community policing methodologies are implemented. If negatrons are allowed to go unchecked, the negative impact they have on the police department will certainly be felt in the community.

Police executives will be addressing new challenges both internally and externally with regard to the way police departments will do business in the years to come. These new challenges during these new times will require police executives to make dramatic and sweeping changes in recruitment procedures, police academy training curriculum, in-service training processes, professional standards implementation, and department management policies.

It will take time and patience to address the challenges we will be facing in the years ahead. Police executives will be successful in implementing new policies via community policing methodologies if they maintain their determination to bring about positive changes.

CHAPTER 3
WHAT HAPPENS WHEN LOCAL GOES GLOBAL

How police in small towns and big cities respond to assignments; how they treat the public; and how they treat each other, has the potential of being seen by millions of people everywhere on this earth.

— LT. STEVEN ROGERS

P olice agencies all across America must be concerned with the image they project to the public. When one police department receives negative press the entire profession suffers.

Illustrations of how far-reaching negative press can have on the image of police departments can be found in the archives of numerous print and electronic media outlets between 1996 and 1997, when the police, nationwide, came under public fire for the way they handled a number of high profile incidents.

The infamous Rodney King incident and O.J. Simpson trial created a national uproar against the Los Angeles Police Department for the methods police officers used to apprehend these individuals and investigate their particular cases. The public outrage against the LAPD was felt by police officers throughout the entire nation.

Another infamous police action during this period of time occurred when federal law enforcement agencies came under tough public criticism for the way federal agents from the ATF handled the standoff of a religious cult leader, at Waco, Texas. Tanks, bombs, and assault helicopters were used to end the siege. Instead of using common sense to address what should have been a local law enforcement matter, overzealous law enforcement officials not living in Waco, lost control of the situation, which eventually resulted in death and destruction.

When police overreact and the result is the destruction of property and the death of innocent people, public confidence in the ability of law enforcement officers to protect our citizens erode and morale in the rank and file of police agencies plummets.

15

From small towns to big cities, police administrators grapple with the issue of *police image*, especially when a high profile incident occurs. It takes strong leadership skills and a plan of action to prevent the loss of public confidence in the police.

Many police executives and patrol officers do not realize the *global* impact their decisions and actions have on the entire police profession.

When serious infractions committed by officers are ignored by police executives, the message communicated to the rest of police personnel is one which is usually interpreted as administration apathy – "If they don't care, why should we care?"

When minor and major infractions are not addressed in a timely manner a negative attitude will spread throughout the entire police department and eventually erode discipline and good order, thus having a profound negative effect on police performance which in turn impacts the public image of the police.

It is imperative that police chiefs and other executives act decisively and swiftly when dealing with problems which have the potential of eroding public and employee confidence in the ability of police department leaders to lead effectively.

In 1995, a case involving two New York City police officers who allegedly beat a dog to death was published in thousands of newspapers across the nation and talked about on nationally syndicated television and radio talk shows. Needless to say, the image of the NYPD was badly damaged, as was the image of police officers nationwide. NYPD Commissioner Bill Bratton got all the facts involving this case and took swift action, firing the officers.

Also in 1995, a police officer from a small police department in the Midwest allegedly beat a Baptist minister with the butt of a shotgun and another officer from the same police department allegedly beat a Catholic priest with a nightstick. When the police chief got all of the facts surrounding both incidents, he immediately fired one officer and suspended the other. Although the rank and file protested the chief's actions, he stood his ground.

The message the rest of the police department received by the swift and decisive action of this chief was unmistakable, compromise your oath of office, and you will lose your job!

In 1997, a number of police officers from a police department in a southeastern American city resisted their chief's new policies which required accountability. Their resistance resulted in the police chief changing command staff personnel, suspending officers who demonstrated habitual behavioral and performance problems, and removing supervisors who refused to support management.

Each *local* problem which surfaced in these law enforcement agencies became *global* for the entire law enforcement community nationwide.

Law enforcement officers should understand that when a police officer from a small town or large city compromises his or her oath of office, the image of every officer in America is tarnished.

Preventing Your Local Problem from Having Global Impact

– Communication Is the Key –

Several years ago, the Kansas City Police Department developed a performance evaluation system which flags police officers who were consistently having problems with their job performance. The system tracked the type and frequency of citizen complaints against officers. Individuals who received three or more complaints against them within a six month period were flagged. Most of the complaints were about the way officers communicated with citizens. Officers who were flagged were required to meet with their division commander who had the authority to schedule them to attend a communication skills course.

Community Policing requires officers to communicate clearly with the general public. Communication is not just "talking to" another person. It includes body language, tone of voice, pitch, and demeanor. Officers who wear leather gloves, mirrored glasses, and other Hollywood type garb will find that the people they meet on the street will be more inclined to speak with a well dressed and more professional-looking officer rather than with them. Hence, the way police officers dress is also a method of communication.

In many cities and towns across the nation police officers are required to learn about the diverse cultures in their community in order to prevent communication breakdowns which have the potential to turn a local minor incident into a "global public image catastrophe" for any police department.

Sometime ago, a newspaper reported that two police officers from a western state stopped a motorist who they believed was a suspect in transporting weapons. After ordering the driver to exit his vehicle, the police directed him to fall to the ground.

Instead of obeying the officer's command, the driver began to run from the officers.

After being apprehended, the driver struggled with the police until he was finally subdued. It turned out that the driver was not the suspect the police were looking for and no weapons were found in the vehicle. In fact, the driver had recently moved to the United States from South America and was known to be a very friendly man in his community.

During a police interview with the driver, he explained that in his former country the police sometimes shoot people when they are ordered to the ground. He thought he was going to be shot when ordered to the ground by these officers.

To the police officers' credit, there was no allegation of excessive force or police brutality. They acted very professionally. One can only imagine how this *local* incident could have become a *global* catastrophe for that police department, had the officers overreacted and used deadly force to subdue the driver.

Learning about the people who live and work in our communities and the communication skills necessary to communicate with them is an important ingredient to a successful community policing program.

CHAPTER 4
BASIC ESSENTIALS

The principal goal of education is to create men who are capable of doing new things, not simply repeating what other generations have done.

— JEAN PIAGET

I t is imperative that leadership from the top down support police-public partnerships by making them integral components of the police department's community policing philosophy.

Each police officer who becomes a leader, such as a first-line supervisor, middle manager, or executive, will develop his or her own management skills to address numerous issues which arise from the implementation of community policing methodologies.

Police executives should convey to every person in the police department what the agency's management philosophy is, and the importance of reviewing and evaluating various management methodologies when implementing and maintaining community policing programs.

Most police executives agree that a key ingredient to successful management is to ensure that individuals who are placed in decision-making positions are well educated, knowledgeable, and experienced.

Unfortunately, many police department executives do not assign the most qualified individuals to leadership positions. In some states, laws which guide promotional appointments, such as in New Jersey, prohibit police executives from appointing the most qualified officers to management positions. In other states, political considerations override public safety considerations when such appointments are made.

In many states, individuals who apply to become a police officer need only to possess a high school or equivalency diploma to qualify for a statewide competitive examination. In many cases, standards are lowered to increase minority participation, and in numerous jurisdictions where there are no state mandated applicant guidelines, politically connected individuals usually get hired regardless of their qualifications.

Lowering professional standards and allowing politics to enter into the recruit selection process has proven to be disastrous for law enforcement.

Police departments that hire unqualified and undereducated men and women run a very high risk of increased civil lawsuits and criminal complaints against police officers who fail to perform their job within the code of law enforcement ethics and federal and state law.

Most chiefs of police are members of a local or state police chief's association. As members of this organization police chiefs are in a position to recommend much needed reforms in the police officer selection process.

As time marches on, it will become necessary for police chiefs and other police executives to collectively raise their voices and address professional standard issues with lawmakers and state police training commissions in an effort to raise police professional standards in the 21st Century. Police executives need to raise professional standards in order to provide avenues for the most qualified individuals to enter the police service.

Model Qualifications

Basic qualification and recruitment standards should require police candidates to have completed a minimum of two years of college or one tour of duty with the United States Military or in civilian public service, such as the Peace Corps, etc.

Additionally, police officers should be required to receive local or state certification in five basic areas; (1) Multi-cultural studies; (2) Secondary language which dominates the officer's geographical location; (3) Family crisis intervention; (4) English composition; (5) Communication skills.

In order for community policing to be effectively integrated into the police department's mission statement, the above areas of study should become part of the agency's performance standards guidelines.

As community policing is integrated into the police department's standard operating procedures, communication skills, mediation skills, and diplomatic skills, will become very important tools for the officer on the street to obtain in order to meet the needs of the public in the 21st Century. Training in these and other subject areas should be continuous throughout an officer's career.

A very valuable resource for police executives seeking to develop professional standards and training guidelines is the Commission on Accreditation for Law Enforcement Agencies (CALEA).

CALEA Training Standard Policy Statement

It is the policy of the "Any Town Police Department" to implement and maintain a comprehensive agency training program for all agency employees. Training has been recognized as one of the most important responsibilities of any law enforcement agency. For these reasons one of the goals of this agency is to provide continuous training for all members of the department. The training function within this department is designed to prepare new officers to conform to the high standards expected of them, to maintain and develop skills of in-service personnel, to provide specialized training for investigative personnel and to provide supervisory and command officers with the skills, knowledge and abilities to perform their assigned tasks. Appropriate training is essential for officers to act decisively and correctly in job-related situations. Training is critical for increased productivity and effectiveness, and ensures consistent performance and unity of purpose, assisting this department to achieve its overall mission.

The purpose of police training and education programs is to enable officers to develop and maintain the knowledge, skills, and abilities required for the effective performance of their duties.

This commission was created "to improve the delivery of public safety services, primarily by: maintaining a body of standards developed by public safety practitioners covering a wide range of up-to-date public safety initiatives; establishing and administering an accreditation process; and recognizing professional excellence."

It would be beneficial to visit www.calea.org for further information about their training programs and professional standards.

Police agencies that adopt CALEA Standards are setting the stage for long-term effective community policing standards which will benefit the entire community for many years to come.

CHAPTER 5
MANAGEMENT METHODOLOGIES

There are police supervisors so preoccupied with their paperwork they never look up from behind their desks to see what's happening on the streets.

— LT. STEVEN ROGERS

D ifferent leaders employ different styles of leadership and management methodologies when implementing community policing programs. The management style a leader may use depends on the crime rate, quality of life issues affecting the community, and the cultural make-up of his or her community.

However, there are common denominators with regard to what management style is best suited to manage community policing programs in differing cities and towns.

Law enforcement practitioners usually employ one of two management methodologies when they implement community policing programs. One methodology is Management-by-Objectives (MBO); the other is Total Quality Management (TQM).

As police departments become increasingly involved in the war on terrorism, there is a third management methodology many police agencies are implementing, which I introduce at the end of this chapter.

Management-by-Objectives (MBO) is a process whereby police executives establish a set of objectives and then convey these objectives to the patrol force.

MBO requires that police commanders and patrol officers agree to what is expected of them with regard to achieving specific objectives established by the command staff, and how these objectives will be achieved. MBO requires very specific planning, time lines, and performance indicators to measure progress.

Many law enforcement practitioners have found that using the MBO methodology to implement and maintain community policing strategies and programs is not effective.

To begin with, there is a general feeling among police practitioners that MBO triggers what can be described as unethical behavior as a result of patrol officers and/or supervisors being

23

pressed by command staff personnel to meet a set of required objectives.

Secondly, events which occur in a community are very fluid. Establishing time lines and performance indicators is counterproductive to the community policing philosophy.

What is a serious crime problem today can be replaced by a more serious crime problem tomorrow, thus causing an entire plan designed to address a specific crime problem to become null and void overnight.

MBO is *performance measured driven* and gives birth to a very dangerous and ineffective leadership style commonly known as "Micro-Management."

Three Pitfalls of Micro-Management

- Micro-management is the least effective leadership methodology when managing police officers working in a community policing environment.

- Micro-managers lack vision and the managerial skills that are necessary to promote teamwork, good morale, discipline and order, initiative and productivity.

- Many micro-managers lead through intimidation and fear and therefore commit a great disservice to their subordinates.

Another leadership methodology used by police management to implement and operate community policing programs is Total Quality Management (TQM).

TQM is fairly easy to implement. Everyday the police chief convenes a Commander's Call with his/her entire command staff. During this meeting, the chief receives briefings on the events which occurred in his or her community over the past 24-hour period. When an unusual or remarkable issue arises, the chief encourages a *bottom to top* review, which requires input from citizens living in specific targeted areas of the community, patrol officers patrolling those areas, and supervisory and command staff personnel. The input sought from the chief includes ideas, suggestions, and proposed solutions to problems surfacing in specific neighborhoods.

Once a number of proposals, ideas, and suggestions are made, the police chief convenes a "huddle group" consisting of command staff personnel. After their review and evaluation of all the input they received, the command staff develops strategic and tactical plans designed to address the problems the targeted area is facing.

When criminal activity in a community becomes very significant, such as a pattern of house burglaries, patrol officers can organize neighborhood huddle groups and solicit direct input from the citizens most affected. TQM gives everyone involved with the problem-solving process a sense of ownership with an opportunity to become a part of the solution.

When community policing is institutionalized as part of police operations, the police organization draws many skills and talents from their employees and the public.

The Benefits of Total Quality Management

- Total Quality Management (TQM) is a leadership methodology that is essential in building trust and a shared ownership of the problems and solutions the police and public face.

- TQM requires police executives and supervisors to spend a good amount of time seeking input from their subordinates and the public in efforts to find solutions to the problems plaguing specific neighborhoods.

- The integration of TQM methodologies into police management strategies serves to prevent both internal and external problems from developing as well as to improve police performance.

- TQM policies are very effective in boosting morale, increasing productivity, and creating an atmosphere of harmony between management and the rank and file.

L-WAID Management Methodology

Many police practitioners are beginning to use the *L-WAID* (pronounced L-WAYED) style of management to meet the new challenges that community policing will be required to address in the years to come.

L-WAID – Leadership With Accurate Intelligence Data – is a leadership methodology and management tool that enables police department decision makers to lead and manage with the best intelligence and information available for pre-operational planning and deployment of police officers into neighborhoods which have specific crime problems and quality of life issues which need to be addressed in the short and long term.

It is a known fact that the side with the most accurate and current intelligence and information about his or her opponent is more likely to be the victor in any conflict.

Police administrators and field supervisors who establish proactive strategies and tactics via community policing should do so only with the most accurate intelligence data available.

L-WAID assures police supervisors that the decisions and plans they will be required to make when addressing specific criminal activity, is based on a corporate knowledge of criminal activity, possible suspects, and the progression of actionable intelligence revealing the criminal intent and potential planning and movements or criminal elements in specific areas of a community.

Effective community policing strategies depend on a wealth of information about *who, what, when, where, why,* and *how,* of every bit of activity taking place in the community.

The best and most valuable "intelligence assets" are the people who live and work in the neighborhoods, as well as the officers who patrol the streets.

A police department with effective community policing strategies will take advantage of such assets.

CHAPTER 6
IMPLEMENTING COMMUNITY POLICING

A journey of a thousand miles must begin with a single step.
— CHINESE PROVERB

The first step police administrators should take when preparing to implement community policing methodologies is to establish a mission statement which clearly articulates the department's goals and objectives.

Administrators should also schedule in-service training and workshops for all police department personnel giving every officer the opportunity to learn about the community policing methodologies and the efforts being initiated by the police administration to institutionalize its concept as department standard operating procedure.

Police personnel should know the nuts and bolts of community policing methodologies; why it is becoming part of their department standard operating procedure; what the police department expects of each officer, and what each officer could expect from the citizenry.

Once personnel throughout the entire police department become familiar with the department's community policing policy, the public must be informed of the philosophical changes the department is making and what impact these changes will have on overall police operations. This is accomplished through the creation of police-public partnerships which are discussed in more detail in a later chapter.

Removing the Police Mystique

When police personnel and the citizens who live and work in the community become familiar with the benefits community policing will bring to them, the police administration must take important steps to eliminate the mystique which defines a number of law enforcement agencies throughout the nation, causing citizens to complain that their police departments are isolated from them.

Many citizens throughout the nation believe that there is a mystique which denies public access to police executives as well

27

as deny the public access to specific information regarding public safety issues which affect their quality of life.

Whether the mystique truly exists or is a false public perception of the police, we have all heard that perception is reality. Hence, we have no choice but to conclude that the mystique the public complains about serves no other purpose but to strengthen the infamous wall of separation between the police and the public.

Citizens who complain about the lack of access to their police department's chief executive officer and his/her staff have a legitimate argument.

Some time ago, I visited a police department where I am not known and asked if I could get information on the crime rate in a specific area of their city. You would think I asked for a mathematical equation to build a nuclear device. Officers scurried to and fro seeking someone to grant permission to release this data. Moments later, a police officer began to grill me as to why I wanted the data, what I was going to with it, etc, etc.

When citizens ask for legitimate information regarding matters which affect their public safety and quality of life, they should be able to obtain it without facing bureaucratic red tape. In order for community policing to work, citizens must be made to feel a part of the crime fighting effort, not apart from it.

When citizens and police work together, the people learn to appreciate the complex job police officers must perform. There are many false perceptions the public has about the police. However, as stated before, perceptions are reality in the eyes of the public. Hence, it is incumbent upon the police agency to overcome such negative perceptions by taking the necessary steps to promote good and effective police-public partnerships, especially via effective and honest communication.

Constructive dialogue between the police department management team, the officers on the beat, and the public is a very important component in turning negative perceptions into positive realities.

Police-Public Dialogue: Model Illustrations

In the late 90s, the Nutley, New Jersey Police Department implemented community policing strategies by first organizing and scheduling a *Town Hall Meeting* between the Chief of Police, his command staff, and the public at large. This meeting was widely publicized as an informal discussion about quality of life and public safety issues affecting the community. The discussion included thoughts and ideas about patrol tactics and policies, crime prevention and current crime issues which affected specific neighborhoods.

The Nutley Police Department learned that the Town Hall Meeting concept was a very effective tool in breaking down the perceived mystique the public had about the police and strengthened positive police-community relations.

During this same period of time, the Montclair, New Jersey Police Department started a program which encouraged citizens to attend certain police department in-service training workshops with patrol officers. The citizens who attended these workshops received an informative education about the pressures and difficulties the police faced in enforcing the law.

Both the Nutley and Montclair Police Departments eliminated the perceived mystique people had about their agencies by opening the door for the public to communicate directly with the decision-makers of the police department.

Organizing the Police Department Town Hall Meeting

There are six steps any police department can implement in planning a Town Hall Meeting:

1. Identify quality of life and public safety issues which need to be addressed.
2. Discuss these issues with the command staff and patrol officers.
3. Schedule your "town hall meeting" at a time and on a date convenient for the public.
4. Publicize the specifics of the meeting in your local and regional newspapers at least two weeks before the meeting.
5. Set an agenda and emphasize that the free and open exchange of ideas, suggestions, and constructive criticisms are welcomed.
6. Ask a citizen from the community to moderate the meeting.

The Chief of Police, the department command staff, and a number of patrol officers should be present at the meeting. The citizen moderator opens the meeting and introduces the Police Chief, who introduces the command staff, and briefly shares the purpose and ground rules of the meeting.

The Chief then discusses current quality of life and public safety issues affecting the community; crime statistics; and other pertinent information. When the Chief completes his/her "report" to the public, the meeting can be opened for public comment.

There are two don'ts to keep in mind when organizing this meeting:

1. If political office holders attend, it is appropriate to introduce them, but *don't* ask them to speak. The presence of politicians tends to politicize the event.

2. *Don't* make any promises to the public. Assure the public that all complaints and concerns will be followed-up. And make sure they *are* followed-up in a timely manner. The credibility of the police department depends upon how and when the police chief and his/her staff react to specific challenges brought to them by the public.

CHAPTER 7
PATROL OPERATIONS

I walk slowly, but I never walk backwards.
— PRESIDENT ABRAHAM LINCOLN

Terrorism and new crime challenges require police departments to re-adjust their patrol operations to maximize police visibility in areas where crime is flourishing.

Along with providing increased police coverage in high-crime areas, better communications with the public and innovative policing methodologies will have to be integrated into strategic and tactical planning concepts in order for the police to be fully effective in addressing quality of life and public safety issues.

Random patrol operations have been the traditional patrol methodology utilized by police departments when deploying officers into the community. However, numerous studies by law enforcement practitioners reveal that random patrol operations are not the most effective means to prevent criminal activity.

Random patrol restricts officers to a reactive patrol mode which limits their contact with the public. Assigning officers to random patrol operations is like putting a sailor on a boat without a rudder. There is no point of reference, no direction, and furthermore a phenomenon known as *tunnel vision* which causes the officer to disregard most of what is going on around him or her. Random patrol discourages officers from conducting minor investigations or initiating positive interaction with the public.

Community policing strategies enable police departments to change from traditional reactive random patrol operations to a more effective *directed patrol* methodology which gives patrol supervisors and officers the opportunity to actively participate in proactive problem-solving policing. This is accomplished through the identification of neighborhood crime and community needs; understanding the quality of life conditions which contribute to these problems; studying problem-solving options and developing long-term solutions to relieve neighborhood problems which are contributing to crime problems; and by initiating community policing methodologies designed to accomplish specific results.

Directed patrol operations are designed to *direct* the police toward specific *targets* which are creating crime problems at specific locations. Increased police visibility, via directed patrol, can be accomplished though foot, bicycle, and motor vehicle patrol.

Community Policing & Patrol Operations

Change never comes easy. There will always be the nay-sayers who resist any new method of approaching crime problems.

Most resistance to community policing methodologies emanates from the rank and file members of the police department because most patrol officers do not understand nor appreciate the virtues of this type of policing.

Resistance to community policing could be reduced and, in some cases, eliminated by using the Total Quality Management (TQM) leadership methodology toward implementation and integration into patrol operations.

The following eight steps are recommended guidelines to integrate and initiate community oriented policing methodologies through patrol operations:

1. The Chief of Police should disseminate a written policy explaining what community policing is, why it is important, and how the patrol force via directed patrol will impact the community.
2. The Chief of Police and his command staff should brief first line supervisors about directed patrol procedures and what results are expected.
3. Once the first line supervisors are familiarized with directed patrol and community policing, they should inform the patrol force of this change in patrol operations, and what is expected of them.
4. Patrol supervisors should assign patrol officers to specific "trouble spots" for the purpose of increasing police visibility as a deterrent to criminal activity. Officers who are not assigned to high crime areas should be encouraged to direct their patrols to locations which they consider to be a

potential problem for the police. Once the directed patrols are observed by the citizens whose quality of life are being affected by active or potential crime problems, the officers patrolling these neighborhoods become their direct conduits to report their concerns and ideas. These officers should be prepared to solve specific quality of life problems on their level, such as if another municipal agency must become involved. Those problems which cannot be solved on the patrol force level would be referred to the agency that can solve them. Nonetheless, whether the problem is solved on the scene by the patrol officer or by the patrol officer making a referral, the fact remains, action must be taken.

5. A "potential problem" is defined as any public concern brought to the attention of the police by the people who live and work in the community. What the police may believe is not a problem, can very well be a big problem for the people who live in a particular neighborhood.

6. At the end of each tour of duty, supervisory personnel should debrief the patrol officers for the purpose of discussing any extraordinary incidents which surfaced during this tour of duty. Officers should be asked to provide feedback on solutions to the problems which the citizens brought to their attention.

7. Once supervisors and patrol officers analyze the problems brought to their attention, and discuss possible solutions, the supervisors should implement an action plan, a solution, and measure its results.

8. In the event a problem brought to the attention of the police needs to reach a higher level of management, an explanation of the problem, along with a proposed solution, should be forwarded up the chain of command to the chief's office for review. After the chief reviews this information with his/her command staff, he should develop a problem-solving action plan with his operations officers and then implement it. This process should take no longer than 48 hours depending on the severity of the problem being addressed.

Back to the 19th Century

Community policing strategies require increased interaction between the police and the public. As stated previously, directed patrols will provide direction and focus on specific crime problems. By integrating directed patrols with foot and bicycle patrols, using a community policing methodology, a very effective patrol operations plan can be created.

During the early days of policing, foot patrols were widely used as a deterrent to crime. It was not unusual to see one and sometimes two patrol officers strolling along city streets. However, with the introduction of high-tech crime-fighting tools, foot patrols were replaced with "robo-cop" policing methodologies which are effective tools in tracking and apprehending criminals, but do little to prevent criminal activity.

Police practitioners generally agree that high-tech equipment is very effective in combating crime from a reactive perspective; but all the electronic gadgets on earth cannot effectively address quality of life issues, racial conflict, economic collapse of neighborhoods, and other root causes of crime problems in our neighborhoods. These problems are left for the patrol officer to deal with.

Many police executives desire to implement foot patrols in conjunction with directed patrol but are unable to do so because of manpower shortages and budget restraints. Simply stated, they do not have the feet to walk the beat.

Numerous police administrators have created innovative ways to complement their community policing initiatives by providing maximum patrol coverage with the minimum resources at their disposal.

Park-Walk-Talk

Once such use of minimum resources many police chiefs have used is to integrate Park-Walk-Talk into their patrol operations.

Park-Walk-Talk is a directed patrol procedure which requires police officers to park their patrol vehicles in the neighborhoods they are assigned to, or at a specific location of their choice, and walk for no less than fifteen minutes at which time they interact with residents, businessmen, merchants, and any other person they come in contact with.

Park-Walk-Talk opens lines of communication between the patrol officers and the people who live and work in the community. This is a patrol procedure which enhances police-community relations and strengthens community policing initiatives.

Vertical Patrol Model

Some police agencies which cover a large number of high-rise apartment or condominium complexes have developed Vertical Patrol methodologies that increase police visibility where large concentrations of people live and work.

- Officers should be furnished with flyers and business cards which they would distribute to apartment or condo residents. This material would explain the Vertical Patrol program as well as provide residents with the officers' names. This component of the program personalizes the policing methodology and helps break down the "police mystique" explained in a previous chapter.
- Officers patrolling specific buildings should encourage public-police dialogue by interacting with residents. When a quality of life or public safety problem is brought to the officer's attention, he/she should take appropriate action and get back to the residents within 24 hours.
- Officers should perform this patrol operation in pairs, and notify their communications center each time they enter a different building, floor, or apartment.
- Vertical Patrols should be conducted at least once a week, per shift, staggering the times.

Directed patrol, foot patrol, bicycle patrol and vertical patrol are community policing patrol methodologies which are designed to enhance community policing initiatives and to prevent criminal activity by:

- Increasing police visibility.
- Offering the public the opportunity to have input in the problem-solving policing process.
- Adding the human component to policing efforts.

Vertical Patrol and the War on Terrorism

With the eyes of the police now focused on potential terrorist activity in their communities, community policing and the patrol procedures integrated into the overall crime-fighting and crime prevention effort can be very effective as illustrated in the following paragraphs.

One month after the September 11th, 2001 attack on New York City, an elderly woman living in a northern New Jersey community reported to her local police department that she observed "something unusual" about her Middle Eastern-looking neighbor. When police investigated, they found that the "something unusual" was something bigger than what they would have ever expected. The following is a summary of what the police learned.

On October 15th, 2001, as two police officers were making their rounds via their Vertical Patrol assignment, a resident on a fifth floor apartment complex approached the officers and told them that early that morning she was walking in the hallway of her apartment building when her neighbor opened his door and exited. She told police that as she said hello to him, she glanced inside his apartment and noticed that there was no furniture. What also caught her attention was a map of the United States on a wall with red marks on it. She stated she would not normally think anything of such a matter except for the fact that her neighbor is of Middle-Eastern decent and the Attorney General was on television the night before asking citizens to report anything they deem to be suspicious. She told police she would not have bothered but since they were in the building, she decided to tell them.

The police learned that the woman's neighbor recently moved to the area from the Middle East. He owned a telecommunications company in New Jersey and had several visitors of Middle Eastern decent visiting him on numerous occasions. Police also learned that when he moved into the apartment complex, he questioned residents about police patrols and neighborhood watch. He owned companies in three southeastern states and was depositing *over $25,000 in cash every week in a local bank. A background check on him revealed information that required the attention of the FBI and INS. Federal authorities continued the investigation and the suspect was subsequently detained. It was later learned that he could have been connected to terrorist activity.*

As a result of initiating the community policing component of proactive Vertical Patrol, the police obtained information that appeared to be linked to terrorist activity.

This incident portrays the importance of community policing as a means to collect critical intelligence and information about criminal activity and more recently, potential terrorist activity.

Unfortunately, not all police departments consider community policing as an effective tool in combating crime.

In February of 2005, a police officer from a northern New Jersey community received a call from a woman who lives in another northern New Jersey community, telling him that she belonged to the police department's community relations Neighborhood Watch program and wished to report suspicious activity in her neighborhood.

She described what the officer believed had the "fingerprints" of potential terrorist activity. The officer advised her to contact her local police department, adding that he was sure they would conduct an investigation.

The next day she called him back and told him that her local police thought she was "nuts" and that no action was taken. The officer was prudent enough to direct her to the FBI. It ended up that this nut came up with some interesting information that may have been related to terrorism.

CHAPTER 8
QUALITY OF LIFE POLICING

Life is not so important as the duties of life.
— JOHN RANDOLPH

In late 20th Century, the New Jersey Police-Community Relations Officers Association, in partnership with the Montclair, New Jersey Police Department, created a community policing strategic plan to improve the quality of life of two Montclair neighborhoods plagued by crime. The plan, named Project Unity, was put into action on April 27, 1997.

Over 200 police officers and volunteers from the City of Montclair and surrounding communities "invaded" two crime-plagued neighborhoods for clean-up. Within several days, two city blocks were transformed from streets and yards littered with debris, glass, trash, broken street lights, run-down housing, and unruly teens hanging out in the streets, to neighborhoods with flower pots, lighting, and well-kept homes. These neighborhoods were taken from the crack dealers and other criminal elements and given back to the people who live and work there.

Unfortunately, as of 2007, these neighborhoods are once again on the decline as a result of a number of reasons.

What we did not know in 1997, we now know in 2007, because we have the opportunity to look back and learn why this success was short-lived. In fact, the answer to the question, "Why was this successful project, so short-lived?" in my opinion was right in front of our faces, we just didn't see it.

One of the glaring things I noticed while helping clean up these neighborhoods was that very few residents who lived in these neighborhoods actually participated in the project.

I took a team of youths from surrounding communities into the backyard of a home which was filled with tires, trash, glass, etc. As we were working very hard through the smells of trash and heat, a young man about 15 years of age came out of his house. I asked him if he lived there and he replied, "Yes." I said, "Here is a shovel; you can help that person over there." He looked at me and replied, "I have to go play ball, they seem to be alright."

There it was, staring me directly in the face, the answer to the question, "Why was this successful project so short-lived?"

Simply put, we did not give *ownership* to the people who live and work in the neighborhoods we were cleaning up. For some reason, many residents who lived in these neighborhoods felt they were entitled to the work being done by others. This is something we did not anticipate but used it as a lesson learned for future planning.

Many psychologists and sociologists believe that lending a helping hand to people who are impacted by crime is not enough to keep neighborhoods safe and secure. What must be included in the planning stages of any project dedicated to clean up neighborhoods from crime are components which are designed to include, as active participants, the people who live and work in the neighborhoods impacted.

I often remember the words of Dr. James Vivinetto, a former assistant superintendent of Nutley, New Jersey, public schools:

> *"In all that we do to help people with the problems they face, we must give them a sense of ownership in the problem-solving process."*

A Dose of Reality

On November 21st, 1996, The National Housing Institute convened a conference headlined: *Strengthening Families and Communities, the Role of Leaders and the Civil Society*. Attending this conference were representatives from several religious, housing, educational, business, government and law enforcement organizations.

The individuals who attended the numerous workshops and meetings during this conference concluded that a majority of people in our society have a strong sense that the core values which bond communities together are eroding; that the character of our civil life is becoming endangered as a result of public apathy, that our political leaders are out of touch with the people who live and work in the community; that the will of the people to volunteer their time to problem-solving is disappearing; and that the institutions which have kept our nation and our families strong are becoming weak and in some cases extinct.

It became apparent to many of the participants listening to the people who live and work in areas of our nation where living with crime is not the exception but the rule, that the cycle of economic erosion, violence, and educational shortfalls has not been adequately addressed by federal, state, or local government agencies.

One observation many of the participants made was that not one elected municipal government official was in attendance. The absence of these officials spoke volumes to the audience.

Politicians will establish committees, make speeches, declare proclamations, make promises and always be available for the photo-op. Here was a real opportunity for many of them to look, listen, and learn about some hard realities people face in our communities, and they simply did not show up.

Interestingly, and with surprise, the people who addressed the crime issues affecting our nation's neighborhoods expressed their belief that the police held the key to a successful campaign in addressing the quality of life problems they faced.

It became apparent that the people lost confidence in their elected officials, and maintained a strong sense of confidence in their local police. This was a dose of reality which embarrassed local government officials but was very welcomed by local police.

Montclair, New Jersey, Project Unity
— Taking Ownership of the Streets Step-by-Step —

On December 19th, 1996, many police executives who attended the November conference sponsored by the National Housing Institute concluded that the people most victimized by crime had given up on their government officials and were now looking to the police for solutions. The goal of these law enforcement officers and others was to help residents who were being victimized by crime, to find solutions via community policing strategies.

With the endorsement and assistance of the Montclair Police Department Chief of Police, *Project Unity* was born.

One asset law enforcement officials had was that the Montclair Chief of Police developed a good working relationship between his department and the people who lived and worked in the community. This relationship would prove to be a major factor toward the successful implementation of Project Unity.

In late December, 1996, I met with the President of the Essex County Association Chiefs of Police and the Montclair Police Chief to discuss the issues affecting residents being plagued by crime. After our meeting, all three of us concluded that crime, like cancer, has a ripple affect that spreads and destroys everything in its path if not treated at an early stage. It was important to develop problem-solving strategies from a multi-jurisdictional perspective if we were going to have a lasting effect on the crime rate. Therefore, we agreed that input should come from police officers and others who not only live in the areas affected by crime, but also from people who live outside the affected areas.

After reviewing a number of problem-solving options offered by police officers and citizens from Montclair and surrounding communities, a steering committee was established and the following five-step problem-solving process was created:

Five-Step Problem-Solving Process

- *Step 1* — To clearly define the "global" problem. In the case of increased criminal activity in Montclair neighborhoods, it was concluded that economic collapse and decay, as well as the diminishing of core values such as pride, character, and unity among residents were major factors which led to crime problems.
- *Step 2* — To refine the *global perspective* to a *local perspective* and target a specific area of the community for problem-solving strategies to be initiated. Two residential neighborhoods near downtown Montclair were selected by the steering committee as target areas to initiate community policing strategies.
- *Step 3* — To select participants for the problem-solving process and to develop goals, objectives, and a mission statement.
- *Step 4* — To develop a community policing and quality of life enforcement strategy for implementation.
- *Step 5* — Implementation.

After this process was established, Mr. Jim Smith and I met in Nutley, New Jersey, on January 12, 1997, to further discuss how best to address the quality of life and crime problems that were going to be addressed in Montclair.

We agreed that the key to success was the creation of a partnership between the police and the people who lived and worked in the area we were going to visit with our community policing team.

However, there was a concern raised by some Montclair residents with regard to how the people in the targeted neighborhoods would receive the police in view of the fact that there had been a barrage of negative publicity about police incidents across the country which was creating tension between the police and the public.

I conceded that there was some merit to this concern. However, I also expressed confidence in the police winning the hearts and souls of the residents once the project got underway.

I convened a meeting with seventy-five police officers on January 16th, 1997, in Nutley, New Jersey, during which time I explained the concept of the project and how a police-public partnership could go a long way in projecting a positive image of the police. The officers enthusiastically embraced the plan and agreed to provide whatever support was needed to assist the residents and the Montclair Police Department in this endeavor.

On January 18th, 1997, Mr. Smith and I spoke about the progress made with the police officers at the meeting held on January 16th. Mr. Smith suggested that we should meet with Mr. Frank Jones of the Housing and Urban Development Organization of Orange, New Jersey. He explained that Mr. Jones is a well-respected individual who has a vast amount of experience related to projects similar to the one we were putting together in Montclair.

On January 21st, the three of us met at Nutley Police Headquarters and discussed numerous issues related to the proposed project in Montclair. We established a mission statement, strategies, and guidelines for the Montclair project. The following mission statement and guidelines can be used by any city or town when developing such a project.

Model Mission Statement

The Any Town Police Department at the invitation of the Main Street Neighborhood Watch Association, will promote and initiate a Neighborhood Oriented Policing Program by visiting 5th Street and 7th Avenue in partnership with the residents of these locations, for the primary purpose of maintaining safe and secure neighborhoods by: (1) Assisting residents make minor repairs to their homes, including installing locks, alarms, and other crime prevention mechanisms; (2) Assist residents in maintaining a safe environment by cleaning and clearing vacant properties; (3) By conducting workshops on empowerment, crime prevention, and on enhancing positive police-community partnerships.

Strategy, Tactics, Guidelines

Key participants in establishing the strategy, tactics, and guidelines for all community policing programs should include the police chief, patrol officers, political leaders, religious leaders, members of the business community, educators, and citizens at large.

Guidelines for Key Participants

1. The **police chief** should select a "targeted neighborhood" based on the quality of life and crime rate.

2. **Police department leaders** should meet with community leaders who live and work in the neighborhoods where the project will commence.

3. **Police and community leaders** should establish a priority list of needs. For example, street lights need repair, abandoned buildings need to be knocked down, etc, etc.

4. **Police and community leaders** should develop a tactical plan designed to address the priority needs established by the group.

After creating these guidelines, the Montclair Police Department Community Policing Bureau established a leadership team consisting of police personnel and city residents. This team met several times and, after evaluating specific community needs, identified critical issues in specific neighborhoods which needed the attention of the police and other government agencies.

The evaluation and conclusions as to what areas of the city would be addressed by the Project Unity coordinators was based on surveys taken by community policing officers.

Captain Dean Reeves, Commander of the Montclair Police Department Community Policing Unit met with city officials and explained to them the details of Project Unity. After his meeting with the city's governing body, he received commitments from the Montclair Fire Department, Road Department, Public Works Department, City Manager, and other key city personnel to join this effort. Additionally, Montclair Police Chief Tom Jordan assigned officers to meet with local business and civic leaders to discuss funding and logistical support. After these meetings, the Salvation Army, United Way, several small businesses, and city clergymen joined the effort.

Also, the New Jersey Police Community Relations Officers Association enlisted the support of dozens of police officers from other cities and towns to support this effort.

On February 25th, 1997, a meeting at Montclair Police Headquarters was held with all the leaders and key participants. The strategic and tactical plans were refined and finalized by the group. Two new components were added to the plan.

First, Reverend Charles Gomez, a local pastor from Montclair, had a congregation located in the middle of one of the neighborhoods affected by this project. He joined the effort and played a crucial role in developing communications between the people and the police. Reverend Gomez also added a spiritual dimension to the project which was applauded by all of the participants.

The second component added was authored by East Orange, New Jersey Police Sergeant James Riley. He suggested that teenagers who are involved in P.A.L., Scouts, Explorers, and other youth groups be invited to participate. His efforts netted the participation of over one hundred teenagers from areas in and around Montclair.

Between February and April of 1997, project leaders worked vigorously to ensure that all the plans developed would be effectively executed.

Project leaders created the following agenda, which was put into action on April 27, 1997.

7:30am: Police personnel, students from surrounding areas, and all participants from Montclair and other areas met at the Bright Hope Baptist Church where Reverend Gomez is Pastor.

8:00am: Reverend Gomez welcomed the 200 participants and led them in an inspirational prayer for success. During this time, Police Chief Ken Starr and Deputy Chief Bill Vaughn also briefed the participants on the operational plan.

8:30am: All the project leaders and participants left the church and reported to a command post which was established between New and Mission Streets.

8:45am: All participants were given their assignments which included minor crime prevention repairs to homes, cleaning up lots, public property, private property, and streets. Vacant and abandoned buildings were knocked down, street light bulbs replaced, and abandoned cars towed away.

12:00pm: Lunch was served to all participants by the Salvation Army, United Way and other business and civic organizations.

1:00pm: All participants met at Reverend Gomez's church where he led a prayer of thanks for a successful day. Chief Starr and his community policing staff presented certificates of thanks to all the participants.

One unplanned event took place at the end of the day. A number of youths belonging to a local gang who congregated on New Street, arrived after the clean up, found their "meeting place" transformed and the neighborhood returned to the residents. These youths quietly walked away and never returned to the area.

Between 1997 and 2000, police increased patrols on New and Mission Streets, and neighborhood watch groups were formed. After September 11, 2001, community policing grants were cut and funding to revitalize neighborhoods were virtually eliminated from the federal and state budgets, thus eliminating community policing programs in several towns and cities.

On February 9th, 2007, I wrote the following column for a New Jersey newspaper and received several calls and letters from people who were impacted by its subject matter.

Citizens Need to Reclaim Their Neighborhoods

There are three basic reasons why cities and towns begin to decline in population and economic growth. First, the "Broken Windows Theory" developed by James Q. Wilson and George Kelling explains the process as to how cities and towns begin to deteriorate, thus negatively impacting the crime rate, property values, and economic development.

Their theory suggests that a specific sequence of events leads up to numerous crime problems and other pubic safety issues which could be prevented if government officials, in partnership with the people, address these events before they lead to more critical problems.

The deterioration of a community begins with accumulated trash, broken windows, uncut grass, deteriorated buildings, and graffiti remaining in neighborhoods for long periods of time.

Unless the decay is treated and stopped, it soon attracts criminal elements, which in turn, discourages economic growth, business opportunities, and a growth in population.

A second reason why cities and towns deteriorate is because of the lack of police manpower and visibility on the streets. When police visibility is reduced, criminals have a greater opportunity to roam the streets and commit criminal acts.

A third reason why cities and towns begin to deteriorate is because their educational institutions are falling apart, physically and academically.

When the mortar and bricks of school buildings begin
to fall to the ground as a result of neglect, academic scores
begin to fall, and attendance begins to decline.

Elected officials who fail to address the critical issues
which result in the deterioration of our cities and towns
place our safety and our future in jeopardy. Citizens who
live and work in these communities feel more vulnerable
and begin to withdraw. They become less willing to involve
themselves with solving these problems because they have
concluded that their elected officials have failed them.

When criminal elements sense this public apathy, they
become bolder and intensify their criminal activity. This
atmosphere attracts more opportunities to commit crime.

The infrastructures of many cities and towns are
falling apart and becoming breeding grounds for drug
activity, gangs, and other criminal elements as a result of
public apathy and political failure. One sure way to
prevent the decline of any city or town is for the people and
their elected officials to address quality of life issues by
maintaining property maintenance codes, supporting
education, and maintaining a strong visible police force.

Dr. James Vivinetto, former Assistant Superintendent
of Nutley Schools once said, "In all that we do, we must
give people a sense of ownership."

The definition of ownership is possession, control.
When criminal elements move into a neighborhood they
take control of every single resident's quality of life.

Citizens can prevent criminals from taking ownership
of their neighborhoods by getting involved and supporting
efforts designed to keep the community safe and secure.

The physical make-up of a neighborhood is a very
important factor in preventing crime. Neighborhoods that
have abandoned buildings, trash in the streets, and run-
down houses, are prime targets for drug dealers and gang
related activity. Hence, citizens have a large stake in
maintaining their property, keeping their streets clean,
and creating an atmosphere which attracts people to live
and work in their neighborhoods.

Last year, residents in a suburban Essex County, New
Jersey town noticed an unusual amount of broken glass,

trash, and other debris scattered all over a children's playground. Several days after noticing this increase in debris, they noticed locks on a lavatory door damaged and the bulbs on street lights broken. The residents discovered that their neighborhood park was being turned into a neighborhood dump where juveniles were drinking and using drugs.

The residents formed a committee which took photos of the park and contacted their local police department. The police department increased patrols, made arrests, and issued summonses to individuals who congregated in the park in violation of local ordinances.

Additionally, the parks department got involved by immediately cleaning up the debris, repairing the damaged rest rooms, and replacing the broken light bulbs.

The residents living near the park formed a Neighborhood Watch group and are now watching the activity in this park every day.

Citizens in every community need to become actively involved in community programs created to prevent criminals from taking ownership of their neighborhoods.

No one can afford to think that these problems are for someone else to address. Government can go only so far in addressing critical problems affecting our way of life. People need to become directly involved.

Police officials across America understand that in order to effectively protect towns and cities from criminal activity, participation of neighborhood residents is essential.

Citizens must keep ownership of their neighborhoods by maintaining a safe and secure environment. This can be accomplished with creating partnerships with the police department and other city or town agencies.

One of the first steps in maintaining ownership of a neighborhood is to develop a Neighborhood Watch program just as the citizens who lived near the park did.

Neighborhood Watch is designed to bring citizens, local government agencies, the business community and others together for the purpose of maintaining a safe and secure quality of life.

With a global war on terrorism in full swing, the need for citizens to become involved in Neighborhood Watch takes on greater significance.

In the 19th Century, Sir Robert Peele, the Father of Policing, stated it is important for the government "to maintain at all times a relationship with the public that gives reality to the historic tradition that the police are the public and the public are the police: the police being only the members of the public that are paid to give full-time attention to the duties which are incumbent on every citizen in the interest of community welfare and existence."

It is incumbent upon every citizen to "police" their neighborhoods and ensure that future generations will have good schools, secure investments, and safe neighborhoods.

Get involved. Call your local police department for information on Neighborhood Watch. The future of this nation depends on what we give up, and what we choose to keep.

CHAPTER 9
AMERICA'S YOUTH AND POLICE

Education has, in America's whole history, been the major hope for improving individuals and society.

— GUNNAR MYRDAL

In the 20th Century, policing methodologies evolved from cops patrolling on the beat, to cops patrolling in police cars, to cops patrolling in the sky and on the sea, and then returning to the beat cop via community policing methodologies.

This evolution in policing went from a period of time when communities enjoyed positive police-youth relations to bad police-youth relations as a result of a combination of national, state, and local issues.

When the United States went to war with North Vietnam in 1964, the way the American people, especially young people, viewed their police changed dramatically.

The war divided the rich and poor, the black man and white man, and ultimately the police and the people. In fact, the war fragmented the relationship between the police and America's youth so badly, name-calling between the two groups turned into violent confrontations.

At the beginning of the Vietnam War, thousands of young American men were drafted into military service. Police departments suffered manpower shortages, forcing them to curtail, and in most cases, totally eliminate the "cop on the beat."

The positive contact beat cops were having with the public was to become a thing of the past. With the disappearance of community policing, went the positive interaction young people were having with their local cops. *Officer friendly* would soon become *officer ugly*.

As the war continued and thousands of American neighborhood boys were being killed in the jungles of Vietnam, the American people began to protest against the government. There was flag burning, riots, and marches all over the nation, mostly organized and led by young people.

The first protests began on college campuses by anti-war students. Soon teachers and professors marched with the students.

Finally, moms, dads, and citizens from all walks of life organized marches against the war in every city and town across America.

When a war is protracted, the first thing that usually suffers is public support. Without the public behind its military, victory will give way to defeat. The Vietnam War lasted ten years, cost 50,000 American lives, became America's first military defeat in history, greatly divided the nation, and devastated the relationship police once had with young people, from coast to coast.

During the 1960s, the friendly cop on the beat with the neatly pressed uniform gleaming in the sunlight, chatting with parents, kids, and shopkeepers, was transformed into the cop wearing a helmet, carrying tear gas, and using physical and deadly force against the very people he/she is called to *protect and serve.*

Many people who witnessed this transformation in policing would not argue that in numerous instances the police had to use aggressive tactics against violent protestors. But the overwhelming majority of Americans saw things differently.

Police officials who believed that get tough policies on protesters would result in a decrease in violence were given a wake-up call when many young protestors began to target them, calling police "pigs," believing that the police represented U.S. government policy toward Vietnam.

Large numbers of America's young people were now at war, not only in the green jungles of Southeast Asia, but also in the asphalt jungles of our nation's streets against another enemy— the police.

In 1968, the Vietnam War was at its peak. During this period of time while tens of thousands of young Americans were protesting against the war, presidential national conventions were being held.

Youth organizations and young people across America who were opposed to the war believed they had an opportunity to make a dramatic change in government policy toward Vietnam by electing a new president and a new Congress to office. Hence, they took their protests from the streets of America to the political party conventions where the presidential candidates could hear first-hand their collective voices in opposition to the war.

The Democratic Party held its national convention in Chicago, Illinois in July 1968. As thousands of delegates attended the convention to nominate a candidate for president, tens of thousands of young anti-war protestors swarmed the streets just outside the Convention Hall in downtown Chicago.

Although there were numerous agitators and instigators looking for trouble, most of the demonstrators were college students, high school students, and parents of men serving in Vietnam.

For the first time since the American Revolution, a cross-section of America's society, representing every religion, ethnicity and economic level, converged on one city, for one cause, at one time.

On the evening of the convention, television news crews began broadcasting numerous speeches from inside Convention Hall. However, rumors were spreading that the crowds outside of the Hall were getting restless. Some news crews covering the events inside Convention Hall decided to go outside onto the streets to see what was going on. Reporters attempting to leave were confronted by Chicago police officers and told they were not allowed outside, and ordered to return to their seats. Arguments erupted and some news reporters ran past the police out onto the streets.

What these reporters observed happening on those streets shocked them. Within minutes of the initial broadcasts of the violence on the streets of Chicago, dozens of news crews were rushing out of Convention Hall, and instead of the convention's "pomp" and "sparkling glitter" being broadcasted worldwide, people were now viewing the American police in action, complements of Mayor Richard Daly and the Chicago Police Department.

Tens of thousands of people were chanting: *"The whole world is watching."* Scenes of police wielding nightsticks on the heads, backs, and legs of men and women, young and old alike, filled television screens. Police were punching kids and dragging them from their cars as viewers watched in horror.

For the first time in American history, with the exception of unwarranted police violence against America's black people, American citizens had come under attack from their own protectors.

Chicago police officials attempted to justify the actions of their officers during hearings and investigations held by numerous government agencies soon after the violence ceased. But citizens throughout the nation who witnessed the carnage and beatings perpetrated by unlawful police actions, did not accept the shallow explanations of Chicago police officials.

The Chicago Police Department sent a chilling and long-lasting message to Americans; especially America's young citizens, that the police in the United States were no longer a friend of the people.

The public backlash against the Chicago Police Department revealed that police in America had lost touch with the public as a result of replacing proactive policing methodologies, with a methodology of policing that isolated the police from the people. The American people would soon learn that police nationwide had embraced an *us against them* mindset.

It took nearly thirty years for America's law enforcement community to publicly admit that some of the Chicago Police Department's actions against the people who gathered in their city during the summer of 1968 were criminal at the very least.

Fortunately, in the 1970s, progressive political leaders and police chiefs throughout the nation knew that something had to be done to change the way the people, especially young people, viewed the police. Many fine police leaders worked hard to re-establish ties with their communities. But in 1973, one tragic incident involving anti-war protestors and the police brought their efforts to a crashing end.

In the early 70s, police and students on college campuses were routinely clashing over the Vietnam War. In 1973, protests got so bad on one college campus that National Guard troops were called to assist the police. Within an hour after the army set foot on Kent State University, several student protesters lie dead on the campus grounds. They were shot down by some of the National Guard troops. An appalled American public blamed the police for this tragic confrontation. It was by far the worst clash between unarmed students and law enforcement ever recorded in American history. As a result of this incident, thousands of young Americans across the nation declared open warfare on the police.

For the next few years, riots, civil unrest, flag burning and police shootings rapidly increased; and news broadcasts carried stories about cops being assaulted, beaten, and shot by young mobs. It was an ugly time of unrest for America.

When the Vietnam War was coming to a close, a new breed of cop was emerging in the police ranks. With peace at hand and better educated men and women joining police departments, the time was ripe to make changes in the way the police in the United States did business. Unfortunately, it would be another twenty years before police officers nationwide would create a more positive image among the youth population.

In the late nineties, the image of the police profession took more devastating blows. Three contributing factors which resulted in the continuous erosion of police-youth relations were: first, law enforcement had to deal with the unjustified criticisms by the news media which continuously sensationalized police actions on high profile cases such as the Rodney King incident and O.J. Simpson Case; second, law enforcement had little or no way to counter the Hollywood characterization of police officers as being an enemy of the public, particularly an enemy of the minority community and young people in general; and finally, perhaps one of the greatest failures of law enforcement was their inability to develop public relations campaigns designed to counter the bad publicity and negative impact which was being portrayed by the media and movie producers, thus causing a rapid evaporation of positive police-community relations in all segments of the population.

In the late 90s, the popular television network, MTV, took a survey of America's youth, seeking their opinions about the police in America. The survey revealed that an overwhelming majority of the nation's young people from ages 13-18 had a negative image of the police.

In an effort to address what was now a global problem police were facing with respect to their relationship with young people, numerous police agencies such as the Nutley, New Jersey Police Department developed Police-School Partnership programs designed to give each group – the police and youth – the opportunity to view the human side of each other.

Before establishing this program, the Nutley Police Department in cooperation with school officials, conducted a survey of high school students asking them how they viewed their local police. Over eight hundred students participated in the survey.

An overwhelming number of students agreed that crime in Nutley was low and that their neighborhoods were safe as a direct result of the Nutley Police Department's crime prevention and community policing efforts, which included rapid responses by the patrol force to emergencies.

Seventy percent of the students surveyed admitted having limited contact (negative and positive) with the police. Not one student complained of excessive use of force, police brutality, racism or prejudicial actions exhibited by Nutley police officers. Most students agreed that officers on the Nutley Police Department treated them fairly.

However, complaints from a number of young people about the negative behavior and bad attitudes demonstrated by one or two officers were constant, legitimate, but not widespread.

Police learned that a very small number of officers needed training in communication skills. What was troubling was that most of the young people judged the entire police department on the way these officers had been behaving toward them.

With the cooperation of school district officials the Nutley Police-School Partnership Program was created to help police bring a more positive image and message to the youth of the community.

Nutley Police Department Police-School Partnership Goals and Objectives

- Increase student awareness and respect for the legal process and law enforcement.
- Demonstrate the role of police officers in the community.
- Present a realistic image of the police, including the "human component" of policing.
- Help students develop an understanding of the concept of justice.
- Open lines of communication between the police and the student population.
- Present a positive image of the police profession.
- Promote awareness and respect for diverse cultures in the community.
- Create and promote violence reduction and conflict resolution methodologies between the police and the student population.
- Promote reduction in bullying and gang-related activity.
- Promote awareness of the dangers of alcohol and drug abuse.

Parents, educators, police officers, elected officials, clergy, and other organizations participated in promoting the partnership. This program transcended from the classroom into the community, thus achieving its desired outcome.

Police-School Partnership Start-up Guidelines

The first step the school resource officer or community policing bureau should take is to attend a minimum of five classes a week at the local middle school. The police officer would initiate a discussion with the students on a topic of their choice. The setting should be very informal. Rearranging the chairs in a circle with the officer sitting in one of those chairs would be a good idea.

After the classroom discussion, the officer should have lunch with the students in the school cafeteria where he/she will be able to continue to interact with them, thus continuing to build a positive relationship.

At the end of the school day, the officer can greet the students who are leaving school, and on days school is not in session, he/she can visit the students in their neighborhoods or at local parks, etc.

The dialogue between the officers and students at their school will help build a positive relationship between the young people of the community and the entire police force. This relationship will transcend into the neighborhoods these students reside in.

Police departments such as the Nutley Police Department, has seen the attitude and behavior of some juveniles whose behavior toward the police were completely negative, change for the better as a result of the police-school partnership program.

As the program in Nutley grew, a number of teachers joined the effort and assisted in organizing after-school clubs and a Junior Police Academy.

Club activities included trips to law enforcement week activities, court houses, and other law enforcement and judicial related functions.

The following survey was completed by Nutley, New Jersey, Middle School Students in 1997, as part of the police department's Police/School Partnership Program.

Sample of Survey Questions and Answers

1. How would you rate the Nutley Police Department? Consider police response time to incidents, crime rate, police-youth relations, police attitude toward the youth of Nutley.

RATING	MALE RESPONSE	FEMALE RESPONSE
Poor	10.5%	6.1%
Fair	38.2%	45.5%
Good	45.6%	45.9%
Excellent	5.5%	2.0%

2. What factor most influenced your answer to question one?

Poor: Negative contact with police, poor police attitude toward youth.

Fair: Various forms of both negative and positive publicity.

Good: Police performance, police visibility, low crime rate.

Excellent: Positive contact with police, all factors stated in "good" category.

3. Do you have any specific complaints about the police?

Male	51.4% yes	48.5% no
Female	48.5% yes	49.1% no

Complaints about police specifically focused on police attitude and behavior when interacting with youth. A large number of youths described some cops as being very negative.

4. *How do you think the police view young people in the community?*

Police don't like youth: Male 67.7% Female: 71.3%

Police like youth: Male 28.6% Female: 32.2%

5. *Have you ever had contact with a police officer?*

Positive: 30.4% male 36.6% female

Negative: 20.5% male 29.2% female

Both: 16.6% male 9.8% female

6. *Are you afraid of the police?*

Yes: 24.0% male 22.4% female

No: 75.8% male 77.5% female

The key to this partnership's success was team work. The Principal of the middle school and one of the teachers worked with the police department to create a model program for other law enforcement agencies and schools to build from.

In the fall of 1999, the American Bar Association, Division for Public Education, published a survey in which over 1,000 students from a wide cross section of the nation participated.

Two questions in the survey were, *"Do you trust the police in your community? Why or why not?"*

These are the responses:

- **Male, 17:** Yes, I do. They seem to be fair to everyone. I have complete trust in all of them.

- **Female, 17:** Yes, I find the police in my community very trustworthy. They have a good reputation and are seen around the community at a lot of public events. They have a new thing where all the police have baseball cards and all the schools have the copies of the cards. I have even taken a self-defense class from one police officer.

- **Female, 18:** The police in my community don't have to deal with as many crises as in other communities, so in that way they aren't as prepared. I believe they do the best they can, but I'm not familiar with many of the police in our area. To solve this problem, the policemen have made up trading cards for the kids so when they get older, they would be more likely to cooperate with the police.

- **Female, 17:** I really have no reason not to trust the police in my community.

- **Male, 17:** Yes, I do. They are pretty good about treating everyone fair and equal, but some people don't like them because they are always in trouble with the police and just don't like them.

- **Female, 17:** Not really. My community is filled with families whose name has a lot of pull with the police. They tend to be prejudiced to the people who don't have the right name. Also our police aren't the smartest people.

- **Male, 18:** I haven't had any run-ins with the police, so I don't have any personal contact with them, but I do feel safe in my community.

- **Male, 16:** I trust the police in my community for enforcing laws. I do, however, sometimes question some of their means for throwing my friends and I out of parking lots because they say that we are loitering. I sometimes think that they have nothing better to do than pick on the youth of the community.

- **Male, 16:** Yes. They help keep things in order, and don't do anything controversial that inhibits our rights. They are stereotypical policemen, but they do a good job. Actually, they are somewhat undermanned, so at times they miss out on drug offenders and small arrests.

- **Female, 17:** Yes, I trust the police in my community. Most of the time I feel safe so I believe the police are doing a good job and can be entrusted with the responsibility of protecting the community.

- **Female, 17:** I do trust the police in our community. They interact with different parts of the community for various things. For example, we have one of the police in our school full time, so therefore we are able to build a good relationship with the officer. I know that some people would not agree because of various reasons but I have never had a problem.

- **Female, 17:** Yes, I trust the police. I say this mainly for the reason that I have never dealt with the police. Therefore, I have to give them the benefit of the doubt and trust them until they give me a reason not to.

- **Male, 16:** I trust the police in my town. I have never had any problems with them but my friends have. Although, my friends usually don't get into serious problems. I do not feel threatened by the police mainly because I hear stories of people getting away with all kinds of illegal activities. Keyser is not that big of a town and doesn't have a big police force. I think Keyser's biggest problem is drugs, and the police can't do much to stop it.

- **Female, 17:** I do trust the police in my community. There really isn't much crime in my community and I see no reason as to not trust the police. The precinct is only a few blocks from my house.

- **Female, 17:** In my town in Maine, there is no police department. The town is small in size and has relatively few criminal activities that occur. I do trust the police in my surrounding communities. I am not a trouble making person and I have never been in contact with the police, except with my school's resource officer. Overall, I have to say that I trust the police. I have no reason not to like them.

- **Male, 16:** I really don't trust anyone for the fact that power corrupts. Especially, in a small town where a few police officers could pretty much do what they want and answer to no one. I have never run into the police so I could care less in a way.

- **Male, 18:** I don't trust the police officers that don't do their job. I feel if your job is to enforce the law then you shouldn't be breaking the law or standing by while other people are breaking the law. Some young people look up to police officers as role models. I know my younger brother looks up to police officers, but if they are breaking the law then young people might think it is okay to break the law. This, of course, is not the right choice. I feel that if you want to eliminate this problem then you should hire police officers that live in the area; the reason for this is that you would have people who really care about what is going on. Also they would have new understanding of what is going on, and know how to stop the problem.

- **Female, 17:** I can say that I trust the police in my town to a certain extent. I feel safe in my town and reasonably protected but the police do conduct unreasonable searches and unlawful traffic stops. The police have shown a significant amount of bias against people driving certain types of cars or listening to loud music while driving. The police may protect my personal safety but the community members may not be subjected to racial profiling but they are profiled in terms of social class and personal preferences.

- **Female, 17:** I trust the police in our area. I think they are fair and honest. They do their job to the best of their ability. The only thing I don't like is, in a small town the police remember everything you do and hold it against you.

- **Male, 18:** No, I do not trust the police one bit in my community. I have a friend who got pulled over a little while ago at the age of 19 and he was intoxicated (I know first-hand because I was hanging out with him that night). The local cops knew the person and they just followed him to his house and there were no tickets given.

- **Male, 18:** Yes, even though some are, undeniably, corrupt, the vast majority put their lives on the line every day for the good of the community.

- **Male, 17:** I have a lot of confidence with the police in my town. Most of them are very involved in the community and have good relationships with many young people in the town. They are all very competent people and are trusted uniformly by the town.

- **Female, 17:** I don't really trust the police in my community because I feel they are after the teenagers and like to start problems. They also never seem to be around when you need them, or if you call for them they will come an hour later.

- **Female, 17:** I trust most of the police in my community. I have to. They are a big part of my security. They are there to serve and protect me and my family. Obviously there are going to be individuals that are unfair and not liked in the police force but that is the way everything goes, including society.

- **Female, 17:** I don't trust the police in my community because, there are times when my alarm goes off and they don't show up to my house like 2 hours after my alarm went off, so if there was robbers in my house they would have gotten what they wanted because the police decided to come two hours later. So I don't trust the police in my community because they show up when they feel like it.

- **Female, 17:** No I do not trust the police. The police will try to manipulate you in a way you don't understand, on the basis that you are still a minor. The police have a little too much power and it is going to their heads. The police, they don't give you RESPECT even when you give it to them. The police don't understand that some people try to keep their cool with them, even when they have a nasty disposition. I feel that the police are not to be trusted on those key points. I have personally been told by a police officer, "most of the people in present day jail are not guilty of the charges brought upon them." That is the stuff right there, that I'm talking about. I feel that I'm actually looking out for you when I tell you these things. In reality, I feel that police should take the feelings of the accused people and show some consideration. I'm coming at you with the truth, based on the personal experience of (one) myself. NO TRUST is what they get!!!!!!!!!!!!!!!!

- **Male, 17:** I would have to say that I do trust the police in my town. I have no basis on which to suspect any misdeeds on behalf of the police. I have had a few experiences with the police myself, and I honestly cannot say they ever acted unreasonably. Instead, they were just doing their jobs. Popular opinion of people my age would not be to trust the police, but they don't understand that 5-0 is just there for our own good, and if they are forced to bust us, it's more than likely because of something we've done wrong.

- **Female, 17:** I trust them to a certain extent. I believe that there is racism involved. I trust that they will do their job in providing me with my due process of law but that they are not doing all they can to protect me and other citizens in the community.

- **Female, 15:** Yes. I have no reason not to. The police in Colorado Springs are nice, but strict at the same time.

- **Female, 15:** Yes. My community is small, and the crime rate is really low.

- **Male, 16:** No one in my immediate family has ever had a problem associated with the police, so I really don't have an opinion related to that. Since this is a small town, there really aren't many crimes that involve mass quantities of police. For the crimes that we do, I think they handle them well. There haven't been any reports of police brutality that I know of and I have never had a bad experience with a cop myself before. So I am pretty comfortable with the police in this area.

- **Female, 17:** No I do not trust any police officer except one. My Uncle Mark. He is the only one I trust. Half of the police around here are worse crooks than the people that they are locking up.

- **Female, 17:** I trust police in our community to protect, but I don't trust them to arrest people who are out there doing bad things. When it comes to them doing their job, it seems that they are more concerned about teenagers and minor offences. They don't really take care of the older people who are doing harsher drugs.

- **Female, 17:** No, I do not trust the police in my neighborhood, because they are just as corrupt as all the hustlers. I once saw a police officer tell them "Guys, go take a walk then come back later when things die down." I know he knew what they were doing and he still allowed them to do their thing without so much as questioning them. I know the game and I know the cops are familiar with it and with the guys that are involved in it.

- **Female, 16:** In one way, no, because they can be harsh. The reason is because I was driving without a license, and my mom was in the car with me. He asked me several questions. He gave me a ticket for $150.00, and said I will see you in court. I went to court and they gave me 2 years of probation.

- **Female, 17:** Yes, we do trust the police in our community, because if there is ever a problem, (accident, house disturbance, etc.) there are at least two cop cars on the spot within five minutes.

- **Male, 16:** I do trust the police in my community, although you don't see too many city police officers around Keyser. You mainly see state police officers because there is a state police barracks no more than 15 miles out of Keyser. The last time I saw a city police officer was when I was in the middle school. They came to teach/inform us on the D.A.R.E program. The officers seemed very kind and gave me no reason to distrust them. As long as I've been living in Keyser (my whole life) there hasn't been high activity of crime, so there is no reason why I shouldn't trust the officers to "protect and serve."

- **Male, 18:** Yes. Although they hassle my friends and I, they are still good cops. They are only doing their job.

- **Male, 15:** I do not trust cops in my community because they always seem to be around when people are doing something minor, but when people are committing a real crime such as stealing from my house they are nowhere to be found. They are lazy, because they do not want to stop anyone for committing a real crime. Another thing I don't like about them is they act like they are better then everyone or like we owe them something.

- **Female, 16:** I do not trust the police in my community, because the police search people without probable cause. The police believe that every black male is dealing drugs. Therefore, the police feel that they have the right to search every African-American. The police are not concerned with a person's safety; instead they are concerned with stereotypes.

- **Male, 16:** I trust the cops that I know. Like if I was confronted by a cop that I didn't know I wouldn't be as kind to one that may live on my street. It's not that I don't like cops because I would do the same thing to a regular person. That's just my view.

- **Female, 16:** I do not trust them too much because so many of them are crooked. They speed all of the time for no reason. Also, when they stop you, it's for something that you did not even do! For example, my mom received a ticket for speeding and not stopping at a stop sign. I was with her in the car and I know that she was not speeding and I know that she did stop at that sign. That wasn't the first time that she's been falsely accused. I would probably trust them if they did their job and did it correctly. But until then – I won't.

- **Female, 16:** No, I do not trust them. They do not distinguish themselves.

- **Female, 16:** At times I do trust police in my community because they do a good job. Sometimes they are not my best people. One time they had a car broke into down the street from my house and they blamed my brother for doing it. They brought him to the station and asked questions. They were told by many people that he was not home that night. Now he is on probation for a long time for something he did not do. In conclusion I feel police do a good job sometimes.

- **Male, 14:** I think for the most part police are trustworthy. I believe it is a select few that abuse their power. There have been studies on this though, and the studies have proven that many people end up abusing their power when put in a position of authority.

- **Female, 15:** One experience we had was when we were coming from Houston and was stopped by police for no reason. He gave us a ticket for speeding, but I trust most of them.

- **Male, 16:** No, I don't trust the police in my community. They don't do their jobs like they say they are going to do. They say their going to patrol the neighborhoods and they ride around for five minutes and leave. When something gets stolen they are not around, but when nothing is happening they take their little five minute ride. I'm not saying I don't trust other police that actually do their job it's just like they send the lazy, non-working ones to our neighborhoods.

- **Female, 15:** Yes, I trust police so far they have not given me the reason not to trust them. I believe that they are doing a

very good job in the community. So far, the crime rate has
gone down.

- **Male, 15:** No, I do not trust the police in my community. I
  believe police are just average citizens who let the government's power get to their heads. Some police corrupt the law
  just as much as other citizens do, which does nothing but
  bring the reputation of our communities down. This is why I
  do not trust police in my community.

- **Male, 18:** I do trust them because they have not given me any
  reason not to trust them. I hope that I can continue to trust
  them just in case one day I might need them.

- **Female, 16:** Yes, I trust, like, certain ones. I feel like certain
  cops are doing a great job, but certain ones aren't. I also feel
  like nowadays they are giving a badge just to anybody. But I
  am not saying that all cops are bad. There are just some that
  make the rest look bad.

- **Male, 16:** I don't know very many of the police in my
  community. However, I trust the ones I know. I trust them
  because I believe in their competence.

- **Female, 17:** Somewhat. The police in our community are very
  open and honest for the most part. For example, one time,
  during the fourth of July, my family and I were using
  fireworks in the street. Since fireworks are illegal for the
  most part in the state of Georgia, one of my neighbors called
  the police on us. When they arrived, the officer asked us how
  our night was going and what we were doing. After openly
  admitting to using fireworks, the officer announced that we
  should be careful, and that it was good that we were in the
  street, away from people's homes and trees. Then he left. If
  other officers treated other offenders like that, then I would
  be skeptical of the police. I guess some laws are enforced
  stronger than others.

Based on the results of this survey and the comments made
by young people about the police, we can conclude that America's
youth, from small towns and large cities, want to have a good

relationship with their local police. Unfortunately, many of them believe that the police are not approachable and therefore are afraid to talk with them. Young people across the nation agree that the police should take a more active role in interacting with them either in school or in their neighborhoods. It also appears stereotyping creates police-youth problems.

For example, many young people believe that when police respond to a street corner to break up a group of teens, they usually assume all of the youths are troublemakers. And on the flip side, all the youths assume all of the cops are harassing them. All agree that the key to building positive police-youth relations is communication.

The following is a list of what some police departments are doing to break down stereotyping and improve police-youth relations.

- Police departments in a number of cities have established "Safe Havens" where police maintain a high profile in an area where youth are more apt to congregate. At these Safe Havens, police provide resources and alternative programs for young people.

- In Columbia, South Carolina, police officers participate in numerous youth activities, school visits, serve as mentors, and co-sponsor social activities such as camping trips, community talent shows, dances, movie matinees, and puppet shows.

- The New Haven, Connecticut, Police Department has established a Board of Young Adult Police Commissioners composed of 26 youth members elected by their peers and appointed by the Mayor. The Board has an office in police headquarters and meets regularly with the Chief to address issues of concern to youth. The Hartford, Connecticut, Police Department has a similar Youth Commission.

- In Somerville, Massachusetts; Ft. Myers, Florida; and Bridgeport, Connecticut; the police run summer programs in which they employ city youths to work along with police in recreational, educational, and safety programs.

- The youth and police in Seattle, Washington, produced *RESPECT*, a handbook distributed to police and youth which focuses on hanging out/loitering and traffic stops.

- The Ft. Myers, Florida, Police Department runs Law Related Education programs to reduce delinquency and improve the student's role as a law abiding citizen for youth at risk of dropping out or being suspended from school. The Jacksonville, Florida, Sheriff's Department initiated its Youth Intervention Program whereby officers meet informally after school with youth from 12-18 to talk, listen, and serve as mentors. Other police departments have created an Adopt-a-Student program which targets youth at risk and provides a police officer for each identified youth as a mentor.

- Australia: Youth participate in Police Open Days organized by the Canterbury Bankstown Patrol. The Police Open Days target students from local high schools. Youth workers talk about issues affecting young people in their area, their service and how they can help.

- Australia: In response to growing concerns in relation to young people in the Wollongong shopping mall, a youth working party was formed. The working party consisted of representatives from local youth services, police and young people. The aim of the working party was to identify issues of concern for young people in relation to youth crime and public space. As a result, the working party has organized a Youth Forum. Young people and representatives from schools, youth services, police, business, council as well as key stakeholders such as the Wollongong City Mall Management were invited to attend. The aim of the forum was to provide an opportunity for all stakeholders to discuss and develop strategies to address public space and youth crime issues. The project has been extremely productive in encouraging an interagency approach to youth issues while developing positive relationships between police, young people, and council and youth services.

When we fail to speak up and speak out, we strike a blow against freedom and decency and justice.
— ROBERT F. KENNEDY

D uring the past few years police departments have been reaching out to the public, seeking their views and opinions about America's law enforcement community from both a global and local perspective.

In the latter part of the 90s two New Jersey Police Departments, Nutley and Wallington circulated a nine-question survey to the residents of their respective communities, seeking their views and opinions on police responses and service.

The survey forms were placed in stores, supermarkets, gas stations, public buildings, and were randomly handed to people walking on the streets and in parks.

Citizens were encouraged to complete the survey and mail it to police headquarters. Both communities received approximately 1,000 responses.

---

*The following is the list of questions the citizens of these communities were asked to respond to by circling one of four responses to each question — **Excellent, Good, Fair, or Poor***

1. How do you rate your local police department?
2. How do you rate the appearance of officers on the street?
3. How do you rate the attitude/behavior of police officers in your community?
4. What do you think is the overall public view of police in general?
5. Have you ever been victimized by a crime?
6. If the answer to question 5 is yes, were you treated fairly?
7. When was the last time a police officer said hello to you?
8. If you ever had an occasion to call the police, did the person who answered the phone act professional?
9. Would you like to see walking patrols in your neighborhood?

The results were tabulated by a local resident and reviewed by each police chief and his command staff. Appropriate action was taken in areas which needed to be adjusted.

The Mount Prospect, Illinois, Police Department conducts a comprehensive citizen survey every three years. The survey focuses on public safety issues, job performance, and police services.

One survey taken a couple of years ago rated police professionalism and service to the community as excellent. The majority of citizens rated crime as low to moderate and expressed a low fear of being victimized by a serious crime.

In 2004, the MPPD distributed surveys in their community newsletter as well as assigned police officers to distribute surveys—in Spanish—to the Hispanic community. Approximately 279 surveys were completed and returned to the police department.

Survey Results

Citizens responding to the survey have lived in Mount Prospect approximately 25 years. Most reside in single family homes, and the rest live in condominiums or apartments.

Approximately 30% had no contact with the police during 2004; 25% had only one contact; and 42% had two or more contacts with the police.

Twenty-five percent of the citizens responding stated they had spoken with a police officer about a matter not related to crime or public safety.

Citizens were asked to give their opinions on police officers' ability, concern, attitude, fairness, and courtesy. Most citizens stated that the police officers of the MPPD were good to excellent in all categories.

In the area of police service, 92% of the citizens surveyed stated police service to the community was good to excellent.

With regard to the crime rate, 69% of the citizens surveyed said crime in their neighborhood stays about the same and about 21% said crime in their neighborhood is up. Overall, the community stated the crime rate is low.

Most citizens stated that they had little or no fear of becoming the victim of a serious crime, while about 49% stated they feared being victimized by a lesser crime.

With regard to the impact community policing had on this community, most residents stated they did not know if community oriented policing had any impact at all on the crime rate.

The results of citizen surveys give local police a good indicator on how well their police department is providing police services to the community and how the people view the police agency as a whole.

There are some State Police organizations that conduct public opinion surveys to see how the public views them and what public safety issues they should be focusing on.

Numerous state police organizations such as the Illinois State Police have updated survey results on the World-Wide Web for public review.

Citizen surveys are very important to police departments seeking to provide the best protection and services to the community they are called to protect and serve.

CHAPTER 11
DIVERSITY, TOLERANCE, AND HATE CRIMES

It is never too late to give up your prejudices.
— HENRY DAVID THOREAU

A hate crime is a criminal act committed against a person because of his/her age, ethnicity, sexual orientation, religious beliefs and numerous other characteristics which motivate a person to commit such a crime.

The 1990 Hate Crime Statistics Act charged the U.S. Attorney General to "acquire data... about crimes that manifest evidence of prejudice based on race, religion, sexual orientation, or ethnicity, including, where appropriate, the crimes of murder, non-negligent manslaughter, forcible rape, aggravated assault, simple assault, intimidation, arson, and destruction, damage or vandalism of property." In 1994, an amendment was added to include disabled people to the list of groups to be tracked.

As of 2007, law enforcement agencies nationwide are seeing an increase in bullying at public schools, which have turned into bias incidents or hate crimes. Children who are obese, wear glasses and who may have a minor handicap have been victimized by such criminal behavior.

In 2005, the U.S. Department of Justice, Office of Justice Programs, published a report revealing some startling facts about hate crimes in America. The following is a summary of the 2005 FBI UCR Report on Hate Crimes.

Bias Motivation

An analysis of data for victims of single-bias hate crime incidents showed that:

- 55.7 percent of the victims were targeted because of a bias against a race.
- 16.0 percent were victimized because of a bias against a religious belief.
- 14.0 percent were victimized because of a bias against an ethnicity/national origin.

- 13.8 percent were targeted because of a bias against a particular sexual orientation.
- 0.6 percent were targeted because of a bias against a disability.

Racial Bias

Among the single-bias hate crime incidents in 2005, there were 4,895 victims of racially motivated hate crime.

- 67.9 percent were victims of an anti-black bias.
- 19.9 percent were victims of an anti-white bias.
- 5.3 percent were victims of a bias against a group of individuals in which more than one race was represented (anti-multiple races, group).
- 4.9 percent were victims of an anti-Asian/Pacific Islander bias.
- 2.0 percent were victims of an anti-American Indian/ Alaskan Native bias.

Religious Bias

Of the 1,405 victims of an anti-religion hate crime:

- 69.5 percent were victims of an anti-Jewish bias.
- 10.7 percent were victims of an anti-Islamic bias.
- 7.5 percent were victims of a bias against other unspecified religions (anti-other religion).
- 4.3 percent were victims of an anti-Catholic bias.
- 4.1 percent were victims of an anti-Protestant bias.
- 3.3 percent were victims of a bias against groups of individuals of varying religions (anti-multiple religions, group).
- 0.4 percent were victims of an anti-Atheist/Agnostic bias.

Sexual-orientation Bias

In 2005, of the 1,213 victims targeted due to a sexual-orientation bias:

- 61.3 percent were victims of an anti-male homosexual bias.
- 19.2 percent were victims of an anti-homosexual bias.

- 15.3 percent were victims of an anti-female homosexual bias.
- 2.3 percent were victims of an anti-bisexual bias.
- 1.9 percent were victims of an anti-heterosexual bias.

Ethnicity/National Origin Bias

Hate crimes motivated by the offender's bias toward a particular ethnicity/national origin were directed at 1,228 victims. Of these victims:

- 58.8 percent were targeted because of an anti-Hispanic bias.
- 41.2 percent were victimized because of a bias against other ethnicities/national origins.

Disability Bias

Of the 54 victims of a hate crime due to a bias against a disability:

- 33 were targets of an anti-mental disability bias.
- 21 were victims of an anti-physical disability bias.

Crime Category

Of the 8,804 victims of a hate crime in 2005, 59.0 percent were victims of crimes against persons and 40.1 percent were victims of crimes against property. One percent were victims of crimes against society.

Offense Type

Crimes Against Persons

There were 5,190 hate crime victims of crimes against persons in 2005. Regarding these victims and offenses:

- Six persons were murdered and three were forcibly raped, each comprising 0.1 percent of hate crime victims.
- 48.9 percent experienced intimidation.
- 30.2 percent were victims of simple assault.
- 20.5 percent were victims of aggravated assault.
- 0.3 percent were victims of other types of offenses.

Crimes Against Property

In 2005, there were 3,530 hate crime victims of crimes against property. Of these:

- 81.3 percent were victims of destruction/damage or vandalism.
- 6.6 percent were victims of larceny-theft.
- 4.7 percent were victims of burglary.
- 4.4 percent were victims of robbery.
- 1.4 percent were victims of arson.
- 0.5 percent were victims of motor vehicle theft.
- 1.2 percent were victims of other hate crime offenses.

Crimes Against Society

Eighty-four victims of hate crimes were victims of crimes against society.

Anyone can be victimized by a hate crime. Victims of bias/hate related incidents go beyond the obvious immediate damage it causes. Individuals who are victimized by a hate crime usually suffer from a wounded psyche which must be addressed immediately by both law enforcement and social services.

Every bias crime victim (hate crime victim) should be treated with the seriousness that the situation calls for. It is imperative that every police officer on patrol keeps their eyes and ears open when interacting with the people who work and live in the community they serve.

Police officers working the streets are in the unique position to learn much about the people they are sworn to protect and serve. The knowledge which can be gained by officers interacting with neighborhood residents can be used proactively to address potential bias incidents and hate crimes.

It is critically important for police officers to avoid tunnel vision when patrolling their neighborhoods. A careful examination of graffiti, vandalism, and other destructive acts can lead to investigations of bias related crimes.

Unfortunately, many television programs glorify hate, bias, and prejudices, especially against young women. The impact these television programs have on young people has the potential to create negative feelings and behavior toward other people in the community.

A 2003 survey conducted by the Canadian Teachers' Federation, identified three major issues related to the impact television has on the behavior of young people toward others.

- Increased fear, also known as the "mean and scary world" syndrome. Children, particularly girls, are more likely than adults to be portrayed as victims of violence on TV, and this can make them more afraid of the world around them.

- Desensitization to real-life violence. Some of the most violent TV shows are children's cartoons, in which violence is portrayed as humorous and realistic consequences of violence are seldom shown.

- Increased aggressive behavior. This can be especially true of young children, who are more likely to exhibit aggressive behavior.

Include ethnicity, religion, and other characteristics which television portrays as different from the rest of society, and you will find that the impact these television programs have on young viewers could be very detrimental to the way they treat others.

One effective method police use to combat the flood of violence and hate being transmitted over the air waves is to educate the public, especially young people, about the effects hate crimes have on an individual victim and the community as a whole.

Police departments throughout America and in other nations are training their officers on methods they can employ to address criminal incidents which stem from biases and prejudices.

For example, police-school partnership programs which highlight the positive characteristics of diverse cultures and emphasize achievements accomplished by people of all ethnic, religious and other backgrounds, is essential in promoting harmony in any school or community.

The Nutley, NJ, police department in partnership with the school district created Operation **A.I.M.** This program underscores the need for young people to identify causes of bias motivated violence and the covert/overt forms of prejudice by heightening their **A**wareness of the problems many people from different cultures face; by encouraging their **I**nvolvement and explaining the important role they have in participating and supporting prejudice reduction programs; and by **M**otivating young people to become involved in eliminating biases and prejudices through education and law enforcement.

The purpose of having a police officer lead the discussion with the students is to emphasize the legal aspects and consequences of laws regarding bias crimes and the important role students can play in assisting the police to prevent violence, hate crimes and other bias related incidents.

Unfortunately, many people, including government agencies turn a blind eye towards bias related incidents. Hence, it is the duty and obligation of the police to keep an open eye on such incidents and, if necessary, take the initiative to right some terrible wrongs.

In 1996, an African-American woman who was the descendent of a well-respected man in a New Jersey community was looking for an apartment for herself and her 12-year-old daughter. After being turned down by a dozen apartment owners, she wrote a letter to the editor of a local newspaper, explaining her dilemma, wondering if her race had anything to do with her failure to find an apartment.

After the local police chief read her letter, police officials took action and within one week found an apartment for this woman and her daughter.

The police department's proactive initiative with regard to this incident conveyed a very clear and unmistakable message to real estate owners in that community that everyone will be treated equal and that the police will not tolerate biases or prejudices in their community.

Civil rights groups, other law enforcement agencies, and human relations organizations praised this police department for the action they took.

The long-term benefits in race relations and police community relations was felt for many years to come as a result of this police initiative.

CHAPTER 12
POLICE COMMUNITY PARTNERSHIPS

People are not an interruption of our business. People are our business.

— WALTER E. WASHINGTON

The following summary lists some community-oriented policing programs police departments across the nation have implemented in partnership with the citizens of their communities.

These programs have proven to be very effective in projecting a positive image of the local police, as well as fostering a good working relationship between the police and the people who live and work in the community being served.

- **PARTNER TO PARENTS:** This program is a New Jersey Police Department's initiative designed to prevent a tragic event from occurring as a result of teen drinking. Partner to Parents is a collaborative effort to help parents provide guidance, education, and safety to their children with regard to the use of alcoholic beverages. The program encourages communication and information sharing between local police and parents with regard to specific teen activities that may encourage the use of alcohol. When parents are away from home and they are concerned that their teenager(s) are going to hold a party, they are encouraged to call the police and let them know what their concerns are. Parents are encouraged to give police permission to stop by their home and visit the teens. Parents are also encouraged to let their teens know that the police will be stopping by for a visit. If the police find illegal alcohol use in someone's home they will notify the homeowners (parents) immediately. If notification cannot be made within a reasonable amount of time, the teens will be transported to police headquarters until notification is made. They will then be turned over to their parents and the juvenile aid bureau will follow-up. In most cases with regard to first-time offenders, the police will not charge the juveniles. However, the decision regarding charges is determined on a case by case basis. The goal of the program is prevention, not prosecution. In addition to educating young people about the consequences of illegal use and abuse of alcohol, police agencies in some communities have created a program to educate adults, especially homeowners, about their liability when alcohol is present at a teen party with or without their knowledge. Once police inform homeowners about *host liability laws* and explain the consequences property owners may reap if minors or even persons within the legal drinking age are served alcohol on their property and serious injury or death occurs, the flow of alcohol is usually prohibited from entering the home.

- **POLICE-BUSINESS ALLIANCE:** This partnership is comprised of local business leaders, retailers and the police. All the participants meet once every three months to discuss the impact certain crimes are having on the economic stability of the community. In some towns and cities across the nation, police-business partnership meetings have served as a catalyst to a number of crime prevention methods suggested to the police by business leaders, resulting in a reduction in criminal activity.

- **POLICE-SCHOOL PARTNERSHIP:** As described in a previous chapter, the Police-School Partnership program encourages classroom activity which includes interaction between the police and student population. These activities can be expanded into the community via after-school programs such as trips to police headquarters, police week activities, police academy programs, the courts, etc.

- **POLICE-CLERGY ALLIANCE:** This partnership consists of local clergy and representatives of the police department meeting quarterly to discuss issues related to domestic violence, family, homelessness, and other social and quality of life issues impacting the community. In many instances police departments have found the local clergy to be a great asset in addressing numerous issues related to public safety.

- **CRISIS MANAGEMENT TEAM:** This team is comprised of community residents who function under the guidance of the police community relations bureau. The purpose of this team is to defuse any potentially explosive issue which can negatively impact the community. For example, a number of communities have created teams of neighborhood residents representing diverse cultures. In the event a racial incident occurs or racial problems involving the police surface, the CMT would be activated to mediate disputes between opposing forces in an effort to defuse potential confrontations.

- **POLICE-FAMILY PARTNERSHIP:** This partnership is comprised of local family members who have suffered the effects of a child or relative who is addicted to drugs or alcohol. Members of this group work with families in crisis through the entire criminal justice process.

- **ASK THE CHIEF CABLE TELEVISION PROGRAM:** Police agencies throughout the nation are utilizing free public access cable television networks to provide the public with a host of public safety and crime-related information. Additionally, a live broadcast gives the chief the opportunity to receive questions and input from viewers about local issues affecting their quality of life.

- **CITIZEN CORPS/NEIGHBORHOOD WATCH:** Citizen Corps/Neighborhood Watch has been a tremendous asset to police efforts in preventing and combating crime. Many citizens organize block parties and host small gatherings at their homes where they invite the local police to discuss public safety issues.

- **APARTMENT WATCH:** Similar to Neighborhood Watch, Apartment Watch includes apartment residents and managers meeting with the police.

- **POLICE-CITIZENS COUNCIL:** This program consists of citizens and police officers meeting quarterly to formulate new approaches toward crime prevention in the community.

- **QUARTERLY PUBLIC AWARENESS MEETINGS:** The police department schedules quarterly public meetings during which time the police chief and his command staff provide the public with an overall view of quality of life, public safety, and crime related issues during the prior quarter.

- **COMMUNITY SERVICE/MENTORING PROGRAMS:** Young people who are taken into custody for minor violations of law are usually sent to a juvenile conference committee or given a station house adjustment. Police are now requiring these young offenders to participate in a community service project such as cleaning parks, helping recruit citizens into neighborhood watch, etc. This program helps mentoring young people and provides them with a constructive program designed to give back to the community.

- **JUNIOR POLICE ACADEMY PROGRAM:** In partnership with the school districts, the courts, the U.S. Military and U.S. Department of Homeland Security, police agencies have developed dynamic programs designed to strengthen police-youth relations.

Junior Police Academy Programs include:

- Crime Scene Preservation/Police Patrol Procedures

- Lessons on Juvenile Laws

- Awareness of the Dangers of Alcohol/Drugs, K-9 Demonstration

- Bullying Issues, Gang Awareness

- Crime Prevention

- Tactical Unit/SWAT Team Demonstration

- Trips to County Police Academy, County Courts, Fire Department, EMS, U.S. Military Bases

---

There are hundreds of programs the police and public can partnership on. Every town and city has its own specific crime problems to address. Hence, the police and the people would need to tailor their programs to meet the public safety demands of their particular community.

CHAPTER 13
VICTIM-ORIENTED POLICING

I have come to realize that in many instances, people who are victimized by crime are also victimized by an insensitive, bureaucratic system of justice.

— LT. STEVEN ROGERS

Violence in America continues to bewilder social science and law enforcement experts. No matter what laws are passed or deterrents to violent criminal behavior initiated, the problem of violence in America continues to grow. And most of the targets of that violence are women and children.

What appears to be of little concern to most American citizens is the fact that the United States of America is finding itself in the midst of a national catastrophe as a result of increasing violence against women and children. This increased violence amounts to what I believe to be the beginning of the total disintegration of our towns and cities.

What is more astonishing than the violence itself is the fact that most of it is being perpetrated in our own backyards. Yet, when police learn of such violence and initiate investigations, many people suddenly become deaf and blind. In other words, they simply do not want to get involved.

The National Organization of Women reveals the following startling statistics on their website:

- **MURDER.** Every day four women die in this country as a result of domestic violence, the euphemism for murders and assaults by husbands and boyfriends. That's approximately 1,400 women a year, according to the FBI. The number of women who have been murdered by their intimate partners is greater than the number of soldiers killed in the Vietnam War.

- **BATTERING.** Although only 572,000 reports of assault by intimates are officially reported to federal officials each year, the most conservative estimates indicate two to four million women of all races and classes are battered each year. At least

170,000 of those violent incidents are serious enough to require hospitalization, emergency room care or a doctor's attention.

- **SEXUAL ASSAULT.** Every year approximately 132,000 women report that they have been victims of rape or attempted rape, and more than half of them knew their attackers. It's estimated that two to six times that many women are raped, but do not report it. Every year 1.2 million women are forcibly raped by their current or former male partners, some more than once.

- **THE TARGETS.** Women are 10 times more likely than men to be victimized by an intimate. Women who are separated, divorced or single, low-income women and African-American women are disproportionately victims of assault and rape. Domestic violence rates are five times higher among families below poverty levels, and severe spouse abuse is twice as likely to be committed by unemployed men as by those working full time. Violent attacks on lesbians and gay men have become two to three times more common than they were prior to 1988.

- **IMPACT ON CHILDREN.** Violent juvenile offenders are four times more likely to have grown up in homes where they saw violence. Children who have witnessed violence at home are also five times more likely to commit or suffer violence when they become adults.

- **IMPACT ON HEALTH AND SOCIAL SERVICES.** Women who are battered have more than twice the health care needs and costs than those who are never battered. Approximately 17 percent of pregnant women report having been battered, and the results include miscarriages, stillbirths and a two to four times greater likelihood of bearing a low birth weight baby. Abused women are disproportionately represented among the homeless and suicide victims. Victims of domestic violence are being denied insurance in some states because they are considered to have a "pre-existing condition."

In addition to these facts, statistics released by the National Center for the Victims of Crime reveal that during the 2003-2004 time period an estimated 896,000 children were victims of criminal behavior, primarily neglect and abuse.

Sixty-one percent of child victims suffered neglect; 19 percent were physically abused; 10 percent were sexually abused; and 7 percent were emotionally or psychologically maltreated.

Additionally, 18.9 percent of child victims experienced abandonment, threats of physical harm, and congenital drug addiction. Fifty-two percent of child victims were girls and 48 percent were boys.

Approximately 40 percent of child victims were maltreated solely by their mothers; another 19 percent were maltreated solely by their fathers; 18 percent were abused by both parents.

The youngest children (from birth through age 3) were the most likely to experience recurring maltreatment.

In the beginning of the 20th Century, an estimated 1,400 children died as a result of child abuse or neglect. Twenty-nine children were murdered by their babysitters in 2003.

If you think these statistics are gut-wrenching, read on. Recently, the Bureau of Justice Statistics released their data on family violence in America.

In the beginning of this century, about 22% of the murders which were reported to police were family murders.

Nearly 9% were murders of a spouse, 6% were murders of sons or daughters by a parent, and 7% were murders by other family members.

Females were 58% of family murder victims. Of all the murders of females in 2002, family members were responsible for 43%. Children under age 13 were 23% of murder victims killed by a family member, and just over 3% of non-family murder victims.

The average age among sons or daughters killed by a parent was 7 years, and 4 out of 5 victims killed by a parent were under age 13. Eight in ten murderers who killed a family member were male. Males were 83% of spouse murderers and 75% of murderers who killed a boyfriend or girlfriend.

The most frequent type of family violence offense was simple assault. Murder was less than half of 1% of all family violence between 1998 and 2002. About three-fourths of all family violence occurred in or near the victim's residence.

The majority (73%) of family violence victims were female. Females were 84% of spouse abuse victims and 86% of victims of abuse at the hands of a boyfriend or girlfriend.

While about three-fourths of the victims of family violence were female, about three-fourths of the persons who committed family violence were male.

The neighborhoods of the 1950s, where the streets were filled with children playing, neighbors smiling, and family members greeting each other, have become streets filled with pain, sorrow, and emptiness.

Police across the nation are doing the best they can to address the needs of crime victims. One program some police departments have established is called Victim Oriented Policing (V.O.P.), a program which is integrated into the police department's community policing approach toward building positive police-community relations by going the extra mile in assisting crime victims.

Victim Oriented Policing is a policing methodology designed to address the needs of crime victims during the immediate and initial contact they have with the criminal justice system via the local police.

Too often police officers arrive at the scene of a crime and become so involved with investigating the elements of the crime, they neglect the human component, i.e. the fact that there are one or multiple crime victims who need attention. V.O.P. is designed to prevent this neglect.

V.O.P. also encourages crime victims to seek long-term solutions to the problems they are facing through a host of referrals which would be made available to them via the officer on the scene.

Police officers who interact with crime victims will be able to utilize local resources for the purpose of initiating a process which leads to the identification of the root causes of certain criminal activity with the purpose of leading to long-term solutions.

In order for V.O.P. to be effective, the police and the community must establish an umbrella organization involving public and private social service organizations, mental health services, family counseling services, religious organizations, and educational services.

Knowledge is power! All the knowledge a police department can obtain about the people who live and work in the community, and the effects of specific crimes, such as crimes against women and children, have on the community as a whole, will be of great benefit toward the implementation of effective community policing programs.

CHAPTER 14
INTELLIGENCE COLLECTION

Knowledge is power.

— SIR FRANCIS BACON

Now more than at anytime in the history of American policing does collecting and analyzing intelligence have greater importance in the process of protecting the public from not only crime in our streets, but also from terrorist activity.

With credible intelligence in-hand, large and small police departments can monitor crime trends and emerging threats which would mandate a change in policing methodologies from a reactionary to a proactive process.

With America at war, police departments are going to have to dramatically increase their intelligence-gathering capabilities in order to protect the population and infrastructure from criminal elements and terrorists.

The first order of business will be for the police and the people to work together in partnership like never before in American history.

In the late 90s, when community policing was the trend of police departments nationwide, the police and the people forged partnerships to address quality of life issues that helped reduce the crime rate. Now, with these community partnerships in place, police agencies can use their relationship with the people as a foundation for what must become their number one policing priority – intelligence gathering.

Historically, there has been no common thread to identify policing priorities and methodologies across the United States. The number one policing priority of every police department differs across the nation. In New York City, the priority the police may be addressing is organized crime. In Chicago, it may be narcotics. In some communities, priorities may range from burglaries to petty thefts. America's police departments must now weave a common thread across the nation that identifies one common policing priority–the defense of the homeland through intelligence gathering and information sharing.

Gathering intelligence on organized crime members is nothing new for police departments. At the very least, most police agencies have some know-how on intelligence collection requirements when investigating organized crime or drug cartel members.

However, there is a vast difference between gathering intelligence on organized crime, drug cartel groups, and suspected terrorist cells. Investigators will have to be trained in new ways to deal with new threats.

Contrary to what some law enforcement practitioners believe, gathering intelligence on terrorists is not that complicated. In fact, it might be easier (in some instances) to gather intelligence about suspected terrorist activity than organized crime members.

Police departments across the United States can collect vital intelligence and information on suspected terrorists by utilizing their partnerships with the people who live and work in the neighborhoods they patrol.

There are three basic steps police departments can implement for intelligence and information gathering of possible terrorist activity.

First – The Chief of Police should create a Police Department Homeland Security Intelligence Bureau (HLSIB). The purpose of this bureau is to collect, analyze, disseminate and take action on any information that may directly or indirectly appear to be linked to possible terrorist activity. Police officers assigned to Homeland Security Intelligence Bureaus can be trained by national law enforcement or military police experts, through numerous government-training programs, including military assistance to civil authorities (MACA).

Second – Once the HLSIB is established, two supervisors should manage the bureau. One supervisor manages incoming and outgoing intelligence and information. He will reach out to citizens who are members of Neighborhood Watch, and provide them with guidelines they can use to keep an eye out for suspected terrorist activity. He can also manage the information the public provides the police and manage the flow of information to and from other law enforcement agencies.

The other supervisor is the "action officer." His job is to make sure action is taken on all terrorist related information flowing into the police department. He tracks investigations, makes sure all leads are followed-up, and works closely with the Federal Bureau of Investigation and other federal law enforcement agencies.

Third – A system to fuse information provided by the public into the HLSIB should be established. Information from the public could be forwarded to the Homeland Security Intelligence Bureau via police reports, the internet, phone calls, or letters.

Most police departments lack the manpower and money to establish individual intelligence units in their police agencies. Police administrators in charge of manpower allocations usually assign a number of their officers to dual roles, spreading their workload as much as possible.

To overcome what may seem to be overwhelming obstacles prohibiting some police departments from establishing new policing priorities designed to meet today's challenges, police departments can assist each other by organizing Homeland Threat Working Groups, comprised of detectives from various police jurisdictions who would network with each other by sharing intelligence and information about specific threats that may impact their individual jurisdictions.

Detectives who specialize in computer crimes, finances and surveillance techniques, should be included in this working group. By sharing these resources, time, money, and manpower would be used more effectively and valuable information would be available for each police department participating in the working group.

The HTWG concept is a good way to provide detectives with a fundamental knowledge of the terrorist cells that may be operating in their area of responsibility. Anti-terrorism experts from the FBI and other law enforcement organizations can provide valuable information about these groups.

Knowing your enemy is vital to addressing potential terrorist activity. When detectives are investigating possible terrorists' operatives, they should know about their training techniques, methods of operation, history and leadership.

This knowledge will help investigators develop unique investigative techniques that will reap valuable information about potential terrorist activity in their community.

Conducting investigations of possible terrorist links to suspicious activity is similar to investigating other criminal activity with one exception. Local police investigators are going to have to rely heavily on federal law enforcement authorities that have the expertise in dealing with the criminal warrior.

Too often police agencies adopt the "protect our own turf" attitude and refuse to allow other law enforcement agencies to interfere with their investigations. The idea behind such a position is that when the "big guy" is captured, the local police department and no one else will get the credit. Likewise, some "feds" play the same game.

In this war, there is no room for egotistical leaders who play games. When local police find a suspected terrorist or terrorist link, they should know enough to call the people who are trained anti-terrorism experts. To do otherwise can result in disastrous consequences. Also, federal authorities should routinely notify local police about terrorist activities that may affect their community.

As of this writing, search and seizure laws, detention laws, and other laws regarding what police can do in the course of an investigation insofar as terrorism is concerned, are being revised. It is imperative that investigators review and learn about the most recent guidelines established by the U.S. Attorney General's office before they begin investigating suspected terrorist activity.

Police-Public Networking

Networking between the police and the public is as important as police sharing information with each other. Police-public information sharing can be achieved through a number of methods within the community policing structure. Crime watch, neighborhood watch, police-citizen partnerships and other programs, which have successful track records in combating crime, can be used just as effectively in combating terrorism.

The key to successful networking with the people who live and work in our communities is linked to keeping police-public lines of communication open twenty-four hours a day, seven days a week.

Once the public is convinced that their local police department is very serious about receiving public input with reference to suspicious activity possibly linked to terrorist activity or crime in their neighborhoods, the wealth of information the police receive may play a major part in preventing a terrorist attack or other criminal activity.

Police officers will have to learn what to look for, what questions to ask, what answers to give, and what information to release to the public. The public will have to learn what to look for, how to communicate what they observe as *possible terrorist activity*, and what not to do when participating as the extended eyes and ears of the police. State and federal anti-terrorism task forces could help local police agencies train and educate the public about their role in this effort.

Police officers generally like to do all the talking when responding to certain incidents. Now they must get used to do a lot of listening and demonstrate a high level of patience when people are giving them information related to the war on terrorism. No small amount of information is insignificant when addressing terrorism issues. Officers must allow everyone offering them information about anything they believe may have a connection to terrorist activity to speak without hindrance.

It is unfortunate that many police officers feel that the public is bothersome at times, or that some information people bring to them is petty. Fortunately, most law enforcement officers on the street are pretty good with the people and work with them no matter how "petty" a matter may seem to be.

Police-public problems usually start with desk officers and dispatchers who are insensitive to public needs. Desk officers and dispatchers can make or break public confidence in a police department by the way they treat a citizen. In this wartime environment, if a dispatcher sends the wrong signal to the public as a result of a negative attitude, the consequences could be deadly.

All the officers in the police department need to understand how important it is to be patient and understanding of someone who offers information they believe to be vital in the war we are engaged in.

Police are going to have to "go the extra mile" to help the public understand that any information they (the public) believe has a terrorist link should be reported. The police will have to convey to the people that if what they report is not linked to terrorist activity, they should not be discouraged from reporting future observations. It is better to report what one might believe to be terrorist related and find out later it is not, than not report a suspicious incident for fear that it will turn out to be nothing, and find out later it was something significant. There is no petty reporting in a wartime environment.

Don't Worry About It—Go Home

A lesson from the failure to network, share, and report critical information was learned the hard way in the early morning hours of December 7, 1941, when two army officers working at a radar station on the Hawaiian Islands spotted hundreds of "blips" on their radar screen.

When they called the watch officer to report what they believed to be very unusual activity on the radar screen, the watch officer told them not to worry. He explained that the blips were probably a squadron of American warplanes returning from a drill. The soldiers replied by telling the watch officer that he might want to check this matter out a little further and make some calls to see if the blips were, in fact, American planes. The watch officer told the soldiers, "Don't worry about it, go home." Twenty minutes later, more than one thousand military personnel and civilians were injured or killed by hundreds of Japanese warplanes, and America entered World War II.

As these soldiers saw the blips on their radar screen, citizens today may see blips on their radar screen when they observe something unusual. It would be prudent for the police not to tell the citizen, "Don't worry about it—go home."

Driving the Point Home

In May of 2007, New Jersey reporters Jeff Whelan, Deborah Howlett, Dunstan McNichol and Wayne Woolley filed a report, which illustrates the need for intelligence collection in partnership with the public. The following is a summary of this report.

Since September 11, 2001, authorities from federal, state, and local law enforcement agencies have encouraged every citizen to become more aware of their surroundings and to report to the police any person or any event they believe to be suspicious, especially if their suspicion rises to a level of possible terrorist activity.

Police department executives understand that the information they receive from the public, no matter how insignificant some of it may appear, may very well turn out to be important pieces of an intelligence matrix they are trying to put together.

One illustration of how important the public is to intelligence gathering occurred in May of 2007, when information given to the police, by a local citizen, lead to the arrest of six Islamic men who allegedly were planning to launch a terrorist attack on the United States Army facility at Fort Dix, New Jersey.

After police began their investigation into this alleged plot, they learned that a number of the Islamic extremists had conducted reconnaissance and surveillance missions at Fort Dix, learning about base operations, police patrols, and other important information related to troop movements and training.

Police also learned that these alleged terrorists also conducted intelligence gathering missions at several other military installations in New Jersey and Delaware. These installations included the United States Army Base at Fort Monmouth, New Jersey; Lakehurst Naval Air Station, Lakehurst New Jersey; the United States Air Force Base, Dover, Delaware;, and the United States Navy Shipyard in Philadelphia, Pennsylvania.

Federal and local authorities believed that the suspects were in the process of planning multiple, simultaneous attacks on these military installations.

According to police reports, the training these men received came primarily from watching videotapes of armed assaults against U.S. military installations. They received their encouragement from viewing movies highlighting Osama Bin Laden encouraging martyrdom.

The police investigation also discovered that these men sought to purchase a number of weapons including assault rifles and explosives.

All the suspects lived what would be called "normal" lifestyles. They went to work, socialized locally, shopped among the local population and had no brushes with the law.

Several young people who attended high school with them told police that some of the suspects were very popular at school and did the normal things kids did during their teenage years.

The suspects' plans were discovered when one of them went to a local store to get a copy of a DVD burned.

A store employee, who was copying the DVD, became alarmed when he observed a group of men (on the DVD) firing weapons and denouncing the United States. He called the Federal Bureau of Investigation and gave them the DVD.

When law enforcement authorities concluded their investigation, the United States Attorney's office filed criminal charges against the suspects.

Another Point Driving Home the Message

On June 1, 2007, four men were arrested for plotting to blow up New York's John F. Kennedy International Airport. These suspects completed pre-operational planning by researching satellite imagery, through reconnaissance, and other means to gather information about JFK Airport and the surrounding area.

In both incidents, the arrests of the suspects were made as a result of the police gathering credible and accurate intelligence.

On June 10, 2007, I appeared on MSNBC to discuss the JFK plot with news anchors. During this interview I explained, *"They are here in the workplace, at our schools, and in our neighborhoods. The American people need to be more aware of their surroundings and be willing to report any suspicious activity to the police immediately."*

CHAPTER 15
AMERICA'S VOLUNTEERS

But where was I to start? The world is so vast. I shall start with the country I know best, my own. But my country is so very large. I had better start with my own town. But my town, too, is large. I had better start with my street. No, my home. No, my family. Never mind. I shall start with myself.

— ELIE WIESEL

President Herbert Hoover was a proponent of supporting volunteers who created public-private partnerships for economic growth and investment. He believed that there were many contributions people could make to strengthen good causes without government involvement.

Today we can follow President Hoover's lead in supporting volunteerism toward police-public partnerships throughout the criminal justice system.

Volunteers can play a critical role in enhancing the image of local police departments, as well as assisting the police in providing more effective services to the public.

Many police departments are finding a wealth of talent within the retirement community. It is here where doctors, teachers, retired law enforcement officers, and other individuals from hundreds of occupational fields could be found to perform important duties in the law enforcement organization.

A tremendous resource regarding volunteering to assist law enforcement can be found on the World Wide Web entitled: Volunteers In Police Service (VIPS). This web page summarizes volunteer opportunities available in law enforcement agencies across the country.

This resource also offers a library of sample documents and forms, including policies and procedures, training materials, and screening forms.

Volunteers in Police Service (VIPS) website offers a resource guide for law enforcement agencies interested in starting volunteer programs.

All of the VIPS resources are geared toward the volunteer. The website also offers:

- Volunteer Programs: Enhancing Public Safety by Leveraging Resources, a resource guide for law enforcement agencies interested in starting a volunteer program.

- A model policy developed in collaboration with the International Association of Chiefs of Police (IACP) National Law Enforcement Policy Center.

- Regional one-day regular training and advanced training providing attendees with the knowledge and skills necessary to implement a law enforcement volunteer program.

- A technical assistance program to help local agencies determine their volunteer needs and design programs that will effectively meet those needs.

- A mentor program that pairs new law enforcement volunteer coordinators in need of support with experienced coordinators.

- Educational videos.

- A monthly electronic newsletter that provides news and events about the VIPS Program and law enforcement volunteer activities across the country.

- A bimonthly electronic newsletter recognizing law enforcement volunteer programs that have recently been in the news.

- A moderated online discussion group for law enforcement volunteer program leaders to share information and ideas.

The VIPS provide support and resources for agencies interested in developing or enhancing a volunteer program and for citizens who wish to volunteer their time and skills with a community law enforcement agency. The program's ultimate goal is to enhance the capacity of state and local law enforcement to utilize volunteers.

For example, volunteers can play a major role in enhancing police operations by organizing a police auxiliary program.

Auxiliary recruits can be solicited by issuing press releases or taking out local newspaper ads; the police public affairs officer could visit local service organizations: PTAs, senior citizen groups; and calling colleges for interns.

Police Auxiliaries could serve as the extended eyes and ears of the regular police force. The men and women who join the police auxiliary can be very instrumental in building bridges between the public and the police by their visibility in neighborhoods where property crimes and other non-violent criminal activity is taking place.

Police Auxiliaries can help establish important community contacts for the regular police force and encourage citizen participation in police-community partnerships. These volunteers can be a vital resource in combating crime and promoting positive police-community relations.

Citizens interested in volunteering to help their police agencies and communities in the war on terror and in preventing crime can log onto *www.citizencorps.gov.*

The following is a brief list of some of the volunteer programs America's Volunteers can become involved with, through their local police agency's community policing initiatives.

- **Citizen Corps Councils** help drive local citizen participation by coordinating Citizen Corps programs, developing community action plans, assessing possible threats and identifying local resources.

- The **Community Emergency Response Team (CERT) Program** educates people about disaster preparedness and trains them in basic disaster response skills, such as fire safety, light search and rescue, and disaster medical operations. Using their training, CERT members can assist others in their neighborhood or workplace following an event and can take a more active role in preparing their community. The program is administered by Department of Homeland Security.

- The **Fire Corps** promotes the use of citizen advocates to enhance the capacity of resource-constrained fire and rescue departments at all levels: volunteer, combination, and career. Citizen advocates can assist local fire departments in a range of activities including fire safety outreach, youth programs, and administrative support. Fire Corps provides resources to assist fire and rescue departments in creating opportunities for citizen advocates and promotes citizen participation. Fire Corps is funded through DHS and is managed and implemented through a partnership between the National Volunteer Fire Council, the International Association of Fire Fighters, and the International Association of Fire Chiefs.

- **USAonWatch (UOW)-Neighborhood Watch** works to provide information, training and resources to citizens and law enforcement agencies throughout the country. In the aftermath of September 11, 2001, Neighborhood Watch programs have expanded beyond their traditional crime prevention role to help neighborhoods focus on disaster preparedness, emergency response and terrorism awareness. USAonWatch-Neighborhood Watch is administered by the National Sheriffs' Association in partnership with the Bureau of Justice Assistance, U.S. Department of Justice.

- The **Medical Reserve Corps (MRC) Program** strengthens communities by helping medical, public health and other volunteers offer their expertise throughout the year as well as during local emergencies and other times of community need. MRC volunteers work in coordination with existing local emergency response programs and also supplement existing community public health initiatives, such as outreach and prevention, immunization programs, blood drives, case management, care planning, and other efforts.

- **Volunteers in Police Service (VIPS),** works to enhance the capacity of state and local law enforcement to utilize volunteers. VIPS serves as a gateway to resources and information for and about law enforcement volunteer programs. Funded by DOJ, VIPS is managed and implemented by the International Association of Chiefs of Police.

- The **Citizen Corps Affiliate Program** expands the resources and materials available to states and local communities by partnering with programs and organizations that offer resources for public education, outreach, and training; represent volunteers interested in helping to make their community safer; or offer volunteer service opportunities to support first responders, disaster relief activities, and community safety efforts.

- **Citizen Corps** is coordinated nationally by the Department of Homeland Security. DHS also works closely with the Corporation for National and Community Service (CNCS) to promote volunteer service activities that support homeland security and community safety. CNCS is a federal agency that operates nationwide service programs such as AmeriCorps, Senior Corps, and Learn and Serve America. Participants in these programs may support Citizen Corps Council activities by helping to establish training and information delivery systems for neighborhoods, schools, and businesses, and by helping with family preparedness and crime prevention initiatives in a community or across a region.

Every American has a duty and responsibility to join the fight against crime and the fight in the war on terrorism. Every American can join this fight by volunteering their time, skills, and talent, to the community policing programs initiated by their local police department.

CHAPTER 16
POLICE-MEDIA RELATIONS

Giving the free press the opportunity to challenge your crime-fighting efforts is a foundational cornerstone of community policing.

— LT. STEVEN ROGERS

D uring the last decade the relationship between police departments throughout the nation and the press corps was very strained. Reporters complained that many police departments were not providing them with complete details about criminal activity in their communities, and police executives were complaining about editorializing or slanted reporting of some reporters who were covering stories related to their law enforcement agency.

For many years police departments kept the press and the public in the dark about crime trends in their community. If a citizen went to their local police department for information related to crime in their neighborhood, it appeared as if they would need a subpoena to get the information.

Years ago, and perhaps today in some communities, crime statistics were "skewed" by police at the request of politicians, real estate brokers, and others to make a specific area of a town or city appear to be very safe. The reason is obvious.

Also, many police departments refused to release crime data such as assaults, thefts, etc, which occurred in schools, in order to maintain a "good image."

One of the most important bureaus in any police department is the media relations bureau. Yet, most police agencies, especially smaller ones, do not have any type of organized media relations standards established for the purpose of disseminating public information and/or interacting with the press.

During the 1940s and 1950s, the police and the press had a very good relationship. In smaller communities just about everyone knew each other, while in the bigger cities, police chiefs socialized with editors and reporters. These relationships somewhat benefitted the police when reporters had to write stories which could either make or break a police department.

As time went on, reporters began to feel the chill from the blue wall of silence and were hard pressed to get information from the police because many police departments isolated themselves from the press corps, failing to provide them with information they and the public were entitled to.

It did not take very long before the police learned that holding important information from the press could backfire. Without accurate information about specific public safety and crime related issues from the police, reporters wrote their news stories with the information they had in hand. This was not a very good arrangement for police-public relations.

As time marched on and police executives began to realize that they needed the press as much as the press needed them, many police departments established media relations bureaus and trained media savvy personnel to become their information officers.

When I became the Nutley Police Department's public affairs officer I felt the "chill" between the police department and the press. Hence, my first objective was to warm the chill and melt the ice.

Within six months I was successful in breaking down that icy wall between the police department and the local press corps. This was accomplished by showing reporters the human component of policing, taking them on a tour of the police department, and then doing what they never expected, schedule weekly press briefings on crime statistics and crime trends, giving them the opportunity to ask questions and challenge our policing methodologies.

Nothing was kept from the press, so long as such information was given to them within legal guidelines established by the Attorney General's and Prosecutor's Office, and that ongoing investigations were not compromised.

During my research on numerous police-press relations programs from throughout the nation, I found that the Iowa City Police Department had a very good set of guidelines published as part of their police department standard operating procedures.

The following is a summary of the media relations guidelines of that department. These guidelines could be utilized by any police department establishing a public affairs bureau.

Media Relations Guidelines
Iowa City Police Department

Policy: It is the purpose of this policy to establish guidelines for release and dissemination of public information to print and broadcast media.

It is the policy of the Iowa City Police Department to cooperate fully and impartially with authorized news media representatives in their efforts to gather factual, public information pertaining to activities of the department, as long as such information gathering does not unduly interfere with departmental operations, ongoing investigations, or infringe upon individual rights or violate the law.

Public Information: Information that may be of interest to the general public regarding policy, procedures or events involving the department or other newsworthy information that is not legally protected, does not unduly interfere with the mission of the department, ongoing investigations, infringe upon the rights of an individual or compromise the legitimate safety and/or privacy interests of officers, victims, witnesses or others.

News Media Representatives: Those individuals who are directly employed by agencies of the electronic or print media such as radio, television and newspapers. Freelance workers in this field are to be regarded as other members of the general public, unless otherwise designated by the Chief of Police or his/her designee.

Public Information Officer (PIO): The department's PIO serves as a central source of information for release by the department and responds to requests for information by the news media and the community.

A. Duties of the Public Information Officer are as follows:
  i) Be present at the scene of major incidents – At the scene of major incidents the officer in charge may designate an area for media to respond and a response route. The PIO will respond to this area and provide information and updates to the media as available.
  ii) Assist the news media;
  iii) Prepare and distribute media releases;
  iv) Arrange for, and assist at, news conferences;

v) Coordinate and authorize the release of information about victims, witnesses and suspects;

vi) Assist in crisis situations within the agency and coordinate the release of authorized information concerning confidential agency investigations and operations.

vii) The Public Information Officer will provide a single authoritative source for media contacts between 07:00 and 15:00 Monday through Friday.

> (1) When the PIO is not on-duty, the Watch Commander will handle media requests. In the event of an incident generating significant numbers of media inquiries, the Watch Commander will determine the need for the PIO to respond.
> (2) Questions regarding an investigation being handled by the investigative section will be handled by the Investigative Supervisor in the absence of the PIO. In instances where the Investigative Supervisor is unavailable, the request will be handled by the on-duty watch supervisor.
> (3) In the event of a prolonged SRT deployment, the SRT commander may request that the PIO respond to a designated location or he/she will designate a person to serve as liaison with the media. The SRT commander may also designate routes by which members of the media should approach the area.

B. Cooperation with the Media:

i) Authorized news media representatives shall have reasonable access to the PIO, the Chief of Police or his/her designee and Command Staff of the department as governed by this policy. When information is denied to a media representative, the basis for that denial shall be fully and courteously explained.

ii) This department recognizes authorized identification from all local, national and international news organizations. Failure of media personnel to present authorized identification may provide grounds for restricting access to non-public information or to incident scenes.

iii) Public information shall be released to the news media and public as promptly as circumstances allow, in as objective a manner as possible.

iv) Public information may be provided to news media representatives and the public by telephone.

v) Ranking officers at crime or incident scenes may release information of a factual nature to the media as governed by this policy or refer the inquiry to the PIO. Where the officer is unsure of the facts or the propriety of releasing information, he/she shall refer the inquiry to the watch commander or PIO.

vi) When an operation involves multiple agencies the agency with primary jurisdiction will make determinations regarding appropriate media releases. The Iowa City Police Department will provide information consistent with this policy when it is the agency with primary jurisdiction. The information should include the identification of assisting agencies.

vii) The Emergency Communication Operator shall inform the Watch Commander as soon as possible upon receipt of information about events or activities that may be of media interest.

viii) The Watch Commander shall be responsible for ensuring that the agency's PIO, Commander of Field Operations and Chief of Police are informed of events that may be of media interest.

ix) Members of the Iowa City Police Department will be consistent in releasing information to the media for public dissemination. A decision to not release normally provided information shall not be solely based on the personal prominence of those involved. Conversely, information that is not routinely distributed shall not be put forth solely as a result of the personal prominence of an involved party.

C. Non-investigative contact with the media is allowed and encouraged. Officers may provide information of a general nature which is not specific to an ongoing investigation.

D. With regard to investigative information from the initial stage of a criminal investigation until the completion of trial or disposition without trial, police personnel should refer requests for information to the Public Information Officer or his/her designee. Upon receipt of the request for information the following guidelines shall be adhered to: *Information that may be released* in connection with an investigation of an event or crime includes but is not limited to:

(1) the type or nature of an event or crime;
(2) the location, date and time, injuries sustained, damages, and a general description of how the incident occurred;
(3) type and quantity of property taken;
(4) information about the victim of a crime;
(5) requests for aid in locating evidence, a complainant or a suspect;

(6) numbers of officers or people involved in an event or investigation, and the length of the investigation; and

(7) name of the officer in charge of a case, his supervisor and assignment. (exception: the name of any undercover officer will not be released).

In instances where the disclosure of the above information may jeopardize an investigation, pose a danger to any person, or is reasonably likely to result in further victimization, the information will not be released. *Information which may not be released* in connection with an investigation of an event or crime, unless authorized by the Chief of Police or his/her designee includes but is not limited to:

(1) the identity of a suspect prior to arrest unless such information would aid in apprehending the suspect or serve to warn the public of potential danger;

(2) the identity of any victim of a crime or any related information which, if divulged, could lead to the identification of victims or witnesses, if such disclosure would jeopardize an investigation to any significant degree, or if it would place any person in personal danger;

(3) the identity of any critically injured or deceased person prior to notification of the next of kin; if a next of kin is not reasonably able to be located, the supervisor of the section conducting the investigation shall determine the method of release of this information;

(4) the results of any investigative procedure such as lineups, polygraph tests, fingerprint comparison, ballistics test or other procedures (the fact that these tests have been performed may be revealed without further comment);

(5) information which, if prematurely released may jeopardize the investigation or interfere with apprehension such as; the nature of leads, specifics of an "MO," details of the crime known only to the perpetrator and the police, or information that may cause the suspect to flee or more effectively avoid apprehension;

(6) information that may be of evidentiary value in criminal proceedings;

(7) specific cause of death unless officially determined by the medical examiner; and

(8) the home address or telephone number of any member of the department.

E. Arrest Information:

(1) Following an arrest, issuance of an arrest warrant or filing for information or indictment, it is *permissible to release*

(a) the accused's name, age, residence, occupation and family status;
(b) the time and place of arrest, whether pursuit or resistance was encountered, whether weapons were used, charges placed against the suspect and description of contraband seized;
(c) the identity of the arresting officers and the duration of the investigation unless the officers are engaged in undercover operations; and
(d) the amount of bond, scheduled court dates and place of the suspect's detention.

(2) Following arrest and formal charging of a suspect, but prior to adjudication, the following types of information *should not be released* without the express permission of the Chief of Police or his/her designee:

(a) Character or reputation of a defendant;
(b) Existence or contents of any confession, admission or statement of a defendant, or his/her failure or unwillingness to make a statement (this does not preclude the release of information that is in the public domain);
(c) Performance or results of any tests, or a defendant's refusal or failure to submit to tests. (i.e. polygraph or voice stress analyzer);
(d) Identity, statement or expected testimony of any witness;
(e) Any opinion about the guilt or innocence of a defendant or the merits of the case;
(f) Any opinion or knowledge of potential for a plea bargain or other pretrial action.

Special Considerations—Criminal Matters: Whether a crime scene or scene of another nature, police have an obligation to preserve the integrity of a scene to gather evidence and for other needed police activities. Therefore, police personnel will delineate the specific scene area and prevent all persons from entering that area for such length of time as there is a need to do so. It may be necessary for scene preservation purposes, and to control general access to the area, to exclude the general public from not only the scene itself, but from a reasonable area around the scene. However, officers must recognize the need for news media representatives to fulfill their obligation to view the immediate scene area for news gathering or photographing purposes. The media representatives will be accommodated, so far as conditions and circumstances permit, to go as near as practicable to the scene itself. News representatives are not to be considered the same as the general public in the area of a scene but rather as persons to be accommodated so that they may fulfill their task.

The news media shall not be allowed access to any area or scene of an incident or crime where there is a possibility that evidence may be damaged, altered, destroyed or otherwise prejudiced by its existence being published or portrayed. Once evidence has been processed, removed or otherwise secured by the department, the media may be allowed to enter by permission of the commanding officer at the scene.

(1) If a police related incident is within a private building, police personnel will secure and protect that part of the building as may be necessary to protect the scene. Under such circumstances all persons may be excluded from the scene until processing is accomplished. If a request is made by a news media representative to enter a building or part thereof, and such entry is not precluded because of police-related purposes, the news representative must obtain permission from the owner or other person in charge of the building or dwelling; if permission is not given and so stated in the presence of police personnel, officers have an obligation to ensure that the denial is honored.

(2) Suspects or accused persons in custody shall not be posed or arrangements made for photographs, telecasts or interviews, nor shall departmental personnel pose with suspects or accused persons in custody.

(3) When an individual is charged with a criminal offense and/or is sought by law enforcement authorities, photographs or mug shots may be released to the media to help locate the individual. No departmental photographs, mug shots, videotape, film or composites of subjects in custody shall otherwise be released to the media unless authorized by the Chief of Police or his/her designee.

Departmental personnel shall extend every reasonable courtesy to news media representatives at crime or incident scenes. Members of the Iowa City Police Department shall not engage in "off the record" comments.

At the scene of major crimes or incidents, such as hostage and barricade situations, the officer in charge shall designate a preliminary press area as early as reasonably possible and as close to the scene as safety and operational requirements allow.

The fact that a suspected suicide has occurred may be reported to the media, along with factual information describing how it happened. The name, age, address, sex and occupation of the victim may also be released following notification of next of kin. The fact that a suicide note exists may also be acknowledged without further comment. The content of such notes is personal and confidential and shall not be released by the Iowa City Police Department.

Special Considerations—Non-criminal Matters: At the scene of significant accidents, man-made or natural catastrophes, the principles of media cooperation shall be maintained to the degree that they do not interfere with the mission of the police, fire, medical or other emergency relief workers.

At fire-related incidents, the decision to allow properly identified news media representatives to pass beyond fire lines or to restrict them from a fire area, will be the responsibility of the on-scene fire commander.

Sensitive information relating to internal investigation of police officers shall not be released without the express permission of the Chief of Police or his/her designee.

Daily activity reports will be made available on a routine basis to media representatives. Statistical data may also be made available to the media. Media representatives are expected to abide by the Code of Ethics published by the Society of Professional Journalists. In the event of a conflict between a member of the Iowa City Police Department and the media, the parties involved are encouraged to bring the concern to the PIO or his/her designee for resolution.

When a representative of the media wishes to speak with an individual officer the request should be routed through the PIO, or when unavailable, the Watch Supervisor. The Watch Supervisor will make the determination as to the availability of the officer; however, to the extent possible, these requests should be made in advance. Officers are expected to cooperate with media representatives to the extent of this policy.

All media questions relating to the policies of the Iowa City Police Department should be directed to the Chief of Police or his/her designee. If questions arise when the Chief or his/her designee is not available, notification of the request shall be forwarded by the Watch Supervisor.

Police-press relations are a fundamental foundation in the community policing process. It is imperative that the police disseminate accurate, credible information to the public as soon as possible via the press and other means. The image and more importantly, the credibility of the police department, is at stake. The pen of a reporter can be used as a positive instrument informing the public with facts, or it can be used as a sharp sword, cutting police-public relations to shreds.

For valuable information and department training with regard to police press relations log onto: www.AmeriCop.org.

CHAPTER 17
AN ABUNDANCE OF IDEAS

Community policing means more than police presence. It means speaking with people who live and work in the community and find out what's important to them, what they want, and try to tailor some police services to meet those demands.
— LA POLICE COMMISSIONER WILLIE WILLIAMS (RET)

C ommunity Policing is a philosophy intended to improve police-community relations by developing partnerships between the police department and the people who live and work in the community. Policing methodologies implemented via the community policing approach gives the citizens at large the opportunity to get to know their police force and to become involved in the law enforcement process through proactive policing initiatives.

Throughout many years, many unwise police administrators and patrol officers have dispelled community policing as "just another program" designed to appease the public. These traditional bound leaders have failed their officers, the communities they work in, and the law enforcement profession as a whole.

It is no secret that police departments cannot, with manpower and budget problems, combat crime on an effective level each police chief would like to attain. However, with public input, involvement, and participation in crime-fighting efforts, the quality of life in each of our neighborhoods could virtually be crime free.

Although there are numerous problems police departments must overcome when initiating community policing methodologies, the most difficult problem to address comes from within the rank and file.

Many police officers are reluctant to embrace this method of policing because it requires them to use skills and talents which they would not normally use in the traditional reactive policing mode.

In the mid-1990s when police departments began to implement community policing methodologies in their communities,

113

one major mistake they made was to compartmentalize the effort by creating community policing units, or teams.

Compartmentalization isolated police officers who were not assigned to community policing units or teams from the community policing philosophy and kept them apart from the community and close to traditional policing concepts these departments were working to replace.

In order for community policing to work effectively, it must not be compartmentalized. It must become a working part of the entire police department, permeating every unit, office, and bureau. Everyone must be a part of the process.

In 1992, the law enforcement publication, Fresh Perspectives, outlined a number of problems police agencies may encounter when implementing community policing as part of the police department's philosophy. These problems included, but were not limited to, overselling community policing as a panacea for every ill that plagues a community: failing to clearly define police service, effectiveness, and problem-solving; creating special units to perform community policing; creating a soft image when addressing crime; isolating the community from the police department.

After addressing problems similar to those listed above, a police department can effectively introduce a host of community policing programs by "thinking outside the box" and bringing the best minds and talents in the community and police department together.

The following is a list of community-based policing programs available on the World Wide Web. Not every program listed may be suited for every police department.

An effective community policing program is tailored to shape police department responses to specific needs in each neighborhood of the community.

• **ACAR: Assigned Community Area of Responsibility.** Uses a self-managed, fixed team of officers who do not have to respond to routine calls for specific service needs.

• **ADOPT-A-COP:** Residency-type program in which community residents get to take care of and know the beat officer like a family member.

- **ARE YOU OK? PROGRAM:** Checks on the welfare of senior citizens once a week.

- **ART PROGRAMS:** Every quarter, the police department displays artwork by juveniles and community residents. Police also organize other art exhibits and local cable access channel coverage. Murals painted in multi-ethnic neighborhoods also work well.

- **ASAP: After School Activities Programs:** Hobby, sports, or other activities. Makes use of school facilities late into evening, sometimes called "Midnight Basketball" programs.

- **AWARDS PROGRAMS:** Special awards given to good citizens who perform honorary deeds or assisted with law enforcement, or were just simply observed displaying good manners while driving.

- **BASIC CAR PLANS:** A type of team policing where the city is subdivided by computer-generated crime occurrence data. A team of nine officers are given 24-hour responsibility for specific subdivision on permanent assignment to develop proprietary interest through formal and informal meetings with the public.

- **BEAT COMMANDER SYSTEMS:** The police sergeant is given command of 20 men including detectives who only investigate crimes in the beat command area on permanent assignment. They are closely monitored for job satisfaction and efficiency at improving citizen satisfaction.

- **BLUE CREW:** Officers who rap, form a band, and throw parties in the community at teen dances or at skating rinks.

- **BOY SCOUT EXPLORER TROOPS:** Special scouting organizations interested in police-related subjects offering escort services, Christmas parties, dinners for those fearful of crime, and ride-along. Almost every big city police department has an Explorer Troop.

- **CAPS: Chicago's Alternative Policing Strategy:** An ambitious program based around monthly meetings between community residents and beat officers; uses problem solving and partnership building as well as involvement with other city agencies to address quality of life issues.

- **CARY: Cooperation for At Risk Youths:** A delinquency prevention program in which police help identify and assess youth who are at risk due to antisocial behavior, drug involvement, gang activity, and/or parental neglect. Police, schools, and counseling centers then jointly co-educate these youths and tailor individualized treatment plans.

- **CAST: Community Action Support Team:** Medical analogy for weed-and-seed type program in which raids and crackdowns are used to break the troubled neighborhood and then anti-drug rallies and other programs help heal or provide the cast.

- **CAT: Combat Auto Theft:** Residents sign agreement asking officers to stop their vehicle if it is being driven during target hours (e.g. 1am-6am). Vehicles have window sticker or other marking to indicate participation in the program.

- **C.C.P.P: Citywide Crime Prevention Program:** Use of block watches, home security checks, and property identification.

- **CITIZEN POLICE ALERT PROGRAMS:** Efforts to involve citizens in reporting suspicious behaviors, finding missing or wanted persons. Similar to block watchers and crime stoppers programs but often including citizen patrols after training and task force formation along with the occasional rewards program.

- **CITY-WITHIN-A-CITY:** A program, in which neighborhoods are rated fragile or threatened, based on infrastructure and housing conditions, and creation of satellite city halls in those neighborhoods to provide better access to city services.

- **CITIZEN SATISFACTION SURVEYS:** Interviews are conducted with citizens randomly selected who had recent contact with the system and asked how well they were served, or alternatively, opinion forms sent out with tax bills.

- **CLERGY-POLICE PROGRAMS:** Central committees of representatives from different denominations established to universally condemn gang violence, for example, and discuss ways police can prevent gang delinquency or recruit people interested in police work.

- **COFFEE KLATCH PROGRAMS:** Two-person teams or a commander who arranges an informal morning or evening of coffee and conversation, with neighborhood residents or elected officials.

- **COMMUNITY ORIENTED SCOOTER PROGRAMS:** Scooter patrol assigned to work with scout cars and connected by CB, and used primarily by campus, corporate, or forestry police.

- **COMMUNITY RADIOWATCH PROGRAMS:** Citizens with CB or HAM radios urged to report suspicious characters and events.

- **COMSTAT: Complaint Statistics:** New technique where weekly community policing meetings are held all around the city, precinct commanders and other police executives are rotated on a regular basis, and immediate accountability is required every 5 weeks from the executives.

- **C.O.M.S.E.C: Community Sector Team Policing:** Decentralized program based on organizational change & community involvement but focusing on index crimes. First developed in Cincinnati about the same time Team Policing was experimented with.

- **COP ON CAMPUS PROGRAMS:** Similar to "officer friendly" programs, but on campus one or two days a week during lunch hours answering questions and discussing issues aimed at students interested in law enforcement careers.

- **C.O.P.E.: Citizen Oriented Police Enforcement:** A program which used door-to-door fear of crime surveys to target problem solving efforts, intensive foot or small vehicle patrol and other door-to-door proactive contacts also used.

- **COPS & JOCKS:** Program that breaks down barriers between high school athletes and law enforcement officers.

- **C.O.R.T.: Community Organizing Response Team:** Police help citizens organize council or block meetings where they devise their own programs.

- **COURTEOUS FIELD INTERROGATION TECHNIQUES:** A type of field training in which non-harassing, courteous, and efficient interrogation is used on suspicious individuals, with officers monitored by supervisor and officers leaving cards bearing their name and badge number.

- **CPOP: Community Patrol Officers Program:** A citizens' patrol program.

- **CPTED: Crime Prevention Through Environmental Design:** Use of security surveys, security devices, lighting projects, landscape design, and other "Target Hardening": sometimes called Operation Safe Streets and by other names.

- **CRIME CONTROL TEAMS:** Decentralized unit relieved of routine, non-criminal duties and given responsibility for controlling serious crime, apprehending offenders, conducting investigations, and increasing clearance rates in a small area of the city.

- **CRIME PREVENTION CLINICS:** Public relations style presentations to encourage preventive steps citizens can take themselves, inform about police services, and promote mutual understanding and cooperation.

- **DANGEROUS TOYS TURN-IN DAY:** Also known as gun buy-back programs.

- **D.A.R.T.: Directed Area Responsibility Teams:** Encouragement of innovation problem-solving with team policing in areas experiencing rapid population growth.

- **DETAIL CARS:** Patrol units not tied to the radio but to the target area, staffed during busiest times of day, to attend scheduled community meetings and make proactive citizen contacts.

- **DIRECTED PATROL:** Called Operation Maximum Effort in some places. Involves patrolling and parking in trouble spots when not committed to other calls.

- **DRUG WATCH:** Like Neighborhood Watch, but citizens usually more active with notepads, cameras, CB radios, or whistles to alert authorities to drug dealing.

- **E.A.R.S.: Enforcement And Rescue Surveillance:** A national group that provides police and paramedic training to citizens who then act as eyes and ears of police and assist with emergency services.

- **FAMILY CRISIS INTERVENTION PROJECTS:** Patrol officers are encouraged and trained in proper skills for dealing with immediate family problems and referring persons in need of assistance to the appropriate agency.

- **FEAR OF CRIME PROJECTS:** Broken windows approach to public incivilities, litter, and nuisances, combined with surveys and/or door-to-door interviews.

- **FOOTBRIDGE PROGRAMS:** New arrivals to city are greeted by uniformed beat officer similar to welcome wagon programs, aimed at elderly who live alone and provides information about city services and crime prevention programs.

- **FOOT PATROLS:** Use of walking beats during all or part of shift, and multi-speed bicycles for silent patrol, better community contact and mobility as burglary-prevention technique in areas not accessible to motor patrol.

- **GANG INTELLIGENCE UNITS:** Inter-agency liaisons often involving citizens, incarcerated offenders, file keeping, and electronic surveillance. Not necessarily CP, but can be part of problem-solving approach.

- **GOTCHA CARDS:** Use of cards left for owners when crime-prone spots are encountered; e.g. "If I was a criminal, I could have entered your house easily..."

- **HIGH INTENSITY PATROL:** An active type of split force policing where some officers disguise themselves as civilians in taverns, for example, and follow or report potential DUI offenders as they leave.

- **HOOD IN THE WOODS:** Outward Bound-type program in which inner-city youths spend time out in the woods to learn social and interpersonal skills.

- **INTERACTIVE COMMUNITY POLICING:** Fully automated process of implementing and evaluating community policing using field laptop computers and a mainframe geo-tracking program formatted for reporting the most commonly performed community policing activities. Activities are rated in terms of public interest, economic development, and overall effectiveness.

- **INTERACTIVE PATROL PROJECTS:** Combining patrol zones on the basis of good or bad relations with police and conducting surveys or experiments to obtain citizen feedback on percep-tions of neighborhood problems; used as citizen input on planning for future patrol tactics.

- **JUST SAY HI PROGRAMS:** Membership cards given to students who wave or yell "Hi!" to police officers as they see them; advertised by popular sports figures, comic or coloring books, often referred to as grin and wave squads.

- **"JUST SAY NO" PROGRAMS:** Use of media role models to get the Partnership for a Drug Free America message out.

- **LANDLORD-TENANT COMPLAINT PROGRAMS:** Specially-trained officers or deputies who deal with rights of individuals in landlord-tenant conflicts, consumer-fraud complaints, and other civil situations who explain rights and procedures to disputants, attempt some mediation, advise consultation with attorneys, and move conflict out of the courtroom.

- **LOFT: Learning Opportunities For Teens.** Recreational and educational activities designed for after school hours, at night, and on weekends.

- **NATIONAL NIGHT OUT:** Once a year, citizens leave outside light on in symbolic unison over need for crime prevention. Tends to involve inter-city competitions.

- **NEIGHBORHOOD ADVISORY COUNCILS:** Community leaders invited or elected to explore community needs and meet with assigned police officers to consider specific patrol tactics and manpower scheduling and to voice complaints and commend personnel.

- **NEIGHBORHOOD POLICE TEAMS:** Similar to beat commander system but with patrol officers taking greater investigative initiative with goal of increased job motivation and quick response time.

- **NEIGHBORHOOD SERVICE CENTERS:** The idea of one-stop shopping for citizens using police substations to serve as alternative to bureaucratic government.

- **NEIGHBORHOOD WATCH:** Police instruction of citizens in home-security measures and enlisting their assistance in watching neighbors' homes; sometimes called block watch programs.

- **OFFICER FRIENDLY PROGRAMS:** Patrolmen with specialized training and skills visit classrooms and other speaking engagements during periods of little activity on shift or during lunch hours, sometimes reinforced by coloring books.

- **OPEN COMMUNITY MEETINGS:** Regularly-scheduled public meetings with prepared agenda and time for general discussion but not a pre-packaged public relations presentation. Often aimed at ethnic communities or neighborhoods.

- **OPEN HOUSE PROGRAMS:** Annual invitations to public to tour offices with special demonstrations of equipment, canine corps, or defense tactics designed to show people that they are welcome and can make friendships, often aimed at university students majoring in criminal justice.

- **OPERATION 25:** Saturation patrol which doubles levels at target times, usually around bars when closing, or at any community nuisance.

- **OPERATION 100:** Violence reduction/avoidance training programs aimed at how to avoid shooting, how to round up illegal firearms (Operation Ceasefire), or how to do more hostage negotiating with offenders. Also a term used to describe drug raids.

- **OPERATION CEASE FIRE:** An anti-gang "hot spot" program aimed at eliminating deaths of young people by guns which taps the knowledge of a wide range of stakeholders, including clergy, community leaders, academics, and gang members themselves.

- **OPERATION CLEAN SWEEP:** Sweeps, raids, jump-out squads aimed at supply reduction in war on drugs targeted to problem street corners, often used with Weed & Seed programs.

- **OPERATION HELP PROGRAMS:** Social worker on police call to help with juvenile problems, provide help with remedial work on socioeconomic problems.

- **OPERATION HOT WHEELS:** Use of stickers saying: "This vehicle paid for by use of seized drug assets" or "confiscated by narcotics unit." They look good in parades.

- **OPERATION IDENTIFICATION:** Police provision of engraving tools and stickers for citizens to mark valuables for burglary prevention.

- **OPERATION NIGHT LIGHT:** An enhanced supervision program involving police and correctional agencies in joint supervision or joint performance of functions such as neighborhood patrols or information sharing for persons on probation or parole and/or gang problems. Police/probation teams go out after curfew in various parks and street corners to demonstrate that probation and police officers are working together.

- **OPERATION NIGHTSIGHT:** Use of loaned, donated, or military-obtained nighttime video surveillance equipment to monitor hot spots or street corners; use of citizens by day to record license plates and use cameras, with or without film.

- **OPERATION PRESSURE POINT:** Reverse buy-bust stings aimed at demand reduction in war on drugs develops list of users and snitches.

- **OPERATION SAFE STREETS:** A weed and seed type program in which police use undercover tactics to remove undesirable people, and then move in with community organizing and development tactics.

- **OPERATION SENIOR SAFE SHOPPING:** Escort services for senior citizens, also called TRIAD programs for the elderly.

- **PACE: Police Assisted Community Enhancement:** Refers to any sort of graffiti removal program where criminal justice employees and citizens work together.

- **PALS: Participate and Learn Skills or Police Awareness Learning Safety:** A family-based program targeting a housing project, recruiting parental talent, and offering 20 or so after-school programs, such as basic skills, sports, music, dancing, hobbies.

- **PARENTAL REIMBURSEMENT PROGRAMS:** Parents reimburse taxpayers for cost of processing and jailing repeat juvenile offenders.

- **PAROLE NOTIFICATION PROGRAMS:** Use of door-to-door flyers or a web site database registry to notify community about returning ex-convicts for certain crimes. Also called sex offender notification programs, or Megan's Law.

- **PATROL ACTIVITY CARDS:** Rural/small town program in which night shift officers leave business cards in residents' newspaper boxes indicating date and time the area was patrolled and that all was quiet, and often combined with Neighborhood Watch on Patrol.

- **PEP: Parent Education Programs.** Monthly meetings in which parents and extended family members of at risk youth participate in analysis of household structures, behavioral management strategies, and citizenship responsibilities.

- **PEPKIDS: Parents, Educators, Police, Kids,** involves a kind of scared straight program where everyone but the kid knows it's a mock arrest.

- **POLICE ATHLETIC LEAGUES:** Volunteer programs in conjunction with boys' clubs or other business/fraternal organizations; solicit funds for baseball, football, basketball, track, boxing, and swimming teams.

- **POLICE-COMMUNITY RELATIONS INSTITUTES:** Week-long meetings with various leaders to discuss in-depth problems; usually held in a university setting as administration of justice or brotherhood week; Public Education activities also called Symposiums.

- **POLICE CORPS:** Federal loan guarantees, modeling after ROTC programs where 4-year college scholarships are offered in return for a 3-year obligation of police service.

- **POLICE MINI-STATIONS:** Establishment of decentralized neighborhood-based precincts in run-down storefronts around the city to guide citizens through bureaucratic maze of municipal government.

- **POLICE-PROBATION-YOUTH DISCUSSION GROUPS:** Informal peer group interactions similar to psychodrama where actual cases are discussed to provide knowledge of law and adequate explanations for police actions in specific incidents so that misunderstandings can be clarified before they become compounded.

- **POLICE TRADING CARDS:** Decks of cards with information about individual officers handed out to 12-year-olds as collectibles and to open lines of communication with youth.

- **POLICE WEEK PROGRAMS:** Annual media events usually sponsored by Concerns of Police Survivors, Inc. and designed to awaken the public to the role played by police in the community; uses tours, talks, and demonstrations; sometimes called Law Enforcement Day.

- **PREVENTIVE PATROL:** Avoidance of predictability, police told to patrol unsystematically to increase visibility.

- **PROBLEM-ORIENTED POLICING:** Use of crime problem analysis, proactive contacts and creative thinking, focuses on community decay and problems that can only be solved using non-arrest options.

- **PUBLIC INFORMATION OFFICERS:** PIOs are assigned full-time to public relations duties, or in small departments as the juvenile officer; they establish police-media guidelines and funnel op-ed pieces to the media. Most of the issues surrounding media relations relate to access and videotaping at crime scenes.

- **PUBLIC RELATIONS PROGRAMS:** Billboards, slogans, bumper stickers, and much more, including programs-of-the-month intended to serve needs of police and information needs of the public.

- **QUALITY SERVICE AUDITS:** Callback programs to users of police services to elicit feedback on citizen satisfaction with services. Often used as part of personnel assignments.

- **RIDE-ALONG PROGRAMS:** Hostile or critical members of community invited to accompany patrol officers to observe the complexities of police work and evaluate the experience, officers, and the department as a whole; often a standard part of university internship experience.

- **ROADS (Realistic Options, Alternatives and Decisions) PROGRAM:** An educational tour which is intended to allow area youth the opportunity to witness first-hand the consequences of criminal activity and the harsh reality of incarceration.

- **SAFE HOUSE PROGRAM:** Houses in high-crime neighborhoods with signs of helping hand in windows where children can duck into in case of trouble or upon seeing suspicious characters.

- **SECTOR PATROL:** Small town program in which the city is divided into sectors based on common attributes such as population density, occupant age, housing style, etc., and an officer is assigned to each sector responsible for holding meetings to identify problems.

- **SENIOR/CHILD I.D. PROGRAM:** Gives citizens a permanent record of identifying information to their family members. The ID card provides fingerprints, height, weight, eye color, hair color, distinguishing marks, and other descriptive information. It is recommended that this card be kept with a family's important documents.

- **SOUND BITE PUBLIC SERVICE ANNOUNCEMENTS:** Efforts to come up with snappy, little sayings that get the police message across, like "You Booze, You Lose" or "Click It or Ticket."

- **SPEAKERS BUREAU PROGRAMS:** Police Department offers a list of different speakers on specialized topics such as narcotics, canine corps, or traffic control for any community group, leaving behind topical pamphlets.

- **SPLIT FORCE POLICING:** Idea of using one portion of force for responding to calls regularly and another portion assigned to directed patrol.

- **STOREFRONT OFFICES:** Use of police mini-stations to reach out and touch the public, often coupled with foot patrol; sometimes used in sting operations where police pose as fences.

- **STRATEGIC PLANNING:** Planning to achieve an organization's potential; is both a document and a process that consolidates the mission, defines new roles for everyone, focuses upon changing the organizational culture, and remains flexible.

- **STREET LIGHTING PROJECTS:** Crime reduction strategies involving citizen-officer cooperation on design and placement of street lights.

- **TALKING CORVETTE:** Police corvette, with car seized from drug dealer that is equipped with tape recorder so passers-by can listen to the story about how the car came into police hands.

- **TALKING MOTORCYCLE:** Police motorcycles equipped with tape recorder in saddlebags, so parked motorcycle can carry on a conversation about cycling safety and the police role to passers-by.

- **TASK FORCE:** Participative, horizontal and vertical planning and team-building process that reduces the traditional distance between ranks and jurisdictions. Solicits street-level ideas and reactions, and promotes organizational change and development; also used to describe various committee formations.

- **TEAM POLICING:** Combining patrol, traffic, investigative operations into teams mixed with generalists and specialists permanently assigned to specific geographic area with total responsibility for crime control, community relations, manpower allocation; wearing of uniforms is often made optional and job titles can be changed to anything the officer wants to be called.

- **TRAFFIC SAFETY AIDES:** Use of trained citizen para-professionals in handling traffic problems, similar to traffic warden programs but no weapons and no responsibility for non-traffic calls; often involves high school students.

- **TRIAD:** A national program bringing law enforcement together with community organizations, businesses, and senior citizens to build partnerships in order to help older adults in two areas: improving quality of life and reducing criminal victimization.

- **URBAN COALITION AND JUNIOR ACHIEVEMENT PROGRAMS:** Inner-city youth summer initiatives for students under 17 and unemployable, who start their own company and function under own management with help of teacher-director.

- **VERTICAL POLICING:** Foot patrol in high-rise buildings. Everyone in the building becomes the eyes and ears of the police department.

- **VICTIM SUPPORT PROGRAMS:** Police-initiated self-help groups, such as "Survivors of Homicide Victims."

- **VICTIM-WITNESS PROGRAMS:** Efforts by police or courts to notify concerned parties about progress and disposition of case; also involves protection, compensation, and referral to other services.
- **VOLUNTEER POLICE AUXILIARY UNITS:** Carefully screened volunteers organized into neighborhood patrol teams to alleviate problems of inadequate manpower; often used at special events such as disasters, riots, or disturbances.

- **VOLUNTEER POLICE ENHANCEMENT UNITS:** Volunteers used to enhance short-handed divisions of the agency, such as school resources, and used to prepare crime info bulletins, document crime trends, process requests for traffic accident reports, provide info on student involvement with crime, analyze false alarms, review 911 calls, monitor noise violations, and assist with data entry and/or centralized records.

- **WEED AND SEED:** Use of operations such as clean sweeps, raids, jump-outs to rid area of drug supply problem, then setting up programs such as ASAP and job fairs to focus on demand problem.

- **YOUNG ADULT POLICE COMMISSIONERS:** Students elected by their respective student bodies serve as police commissioners, are sworn in by the mayor, and meet monthly with city officials.

- **YOUTH SERVICE BUREAUS:** Diversion programs for youths in trouble who need social services, employment, training, education, housing medical care, family counseling, psychiatric care, or welfare; should be voluntary participation and not coercive mandate or part of probation surveillance.

As stated earlier in this chapter, anyone of these programs can be tailored to meet the needs of any police department initiating a community policing program. All of them have a proven track record of working.

CHAPTER 18
CONFLICT RESOLUTION

*The organization chart basically shows you the formal rules.
But the ropes of the organization, how it actually works, is the
human network.*

— THORNTON MAY

E very community has its fair share of conflicts. From
domestic violence to neighborhood disputes, the police
are called upon to mediate, counsel, and resolve most of
the problems people are locked in combat over.

In November of 1997, the Nutley, New Jersey Police Department's community policing efforts paid big dividends in an area
of the township where an explosive situation was developing
between a number of local business owners.

The following summary explaining some elements of this
conflict could serve as a "conflict resolution" model for other
police agencies to use when addressing community conflicts.

Business owners in the area of Bloomfield Avenue and High
Street had been negatively impacted because of the lack of
customer parking. Some business owners claimed that residents
were parking their vehicles in spaces which were supposed to be
used by customers. This problem escalated into a situation which
required police intervention in enforcing existing laws and
mediation of the disputing parties.

Specifically, the target area the police needed to address was
the north and south side of High Street, between Funston Place
and Bloomfield Ave., a mix of businesses and single family homes.

On the north side of High Street sits a dentist's office, hairdresser, tailor shop and seat cover business. On the south side of
High Street exists a delicatessen, vacuum cleaner repair shop,
and a small retail shop.

There are five parking meters in front of businesses on the
north side of High Street and in front of the businesses on the
south side of High Street parking is prohibited.

As a result of the escalating problems between the business
owners and the residents, the business owners requested the
intervention of the Nutley Police Department.

Two officers who were specifically assigned as mediators had solicited the assistance of a well respected citizen, Mr. Walter Smith. The officers requested that Mr. Smith convene a meeting of all interested parties for the purpose of mediating between the disputing parties; and to seek a satisfactory solution that all parties could live with.

During the meeting it was determined that the hairdresser has a high volume of business which requires customers to park long-term (up to three hours) in the target area. The long-term parking negatively impacted the businesses which required short-term parking for their customers.

It was also discovered that police enforcement of existing parking laws was inconsistent; that the meters reflected a three-hour parking limit whereas municipal parking signs indicate a one-hour parking limit; and dozens of vehicles belonging to individuals who are employed at a large corporation in the area, parked in the only available parking spaces for up to eight hours, thus totally eliminating all legal parking in the area.

After several hours of discussion, a solution to this problem was arrived at through the participation of all parties involved.

(1) That five meters in the target area which allow for long-term parking be replaced with meters or signs which reflect either 15 or 30 minute parking. Since meters are not installed for revenue purposes and to ensure a reasonable turnover rate for small business owners, a local ordinance reflecting this change would be attainable.

(2) That approximately 200 feet of Funston Place, (north from High Street) become an unlimited time parking area. This area of Funston Place has no homes or businesses bordering the street and therefore no one would be negatively impacted.

(3) In order to ensure that each recommendation serves its intended purpose, the police department would implement directed patrols and foot patrols via its *park and walk* initiative, in the targeted area for the purpose of monitoring the situation.

The process in which this conflict was resolved brought to surface the spirit of what community policing is all about. The police utilized the talents of a well-respected businessman to chair the meeting and created an environment where all the participants obtain ownership of the problem as well as the solution.

In an effort to be proactive with regard to neighborhood conflicts or conflicts which can surface as a result of a police action, many police departments are creating crisis intervention teams comprised of residents, clergy, businessmen and women, and other community minded individuals from all walks of life, who are willing to volunteer their time to defuse any potential crisis facing the community through negotiation and mediation.

For more information about creating a Crisis Intervention Team, contact AmeriCopUSA at: www.AmeriCop.org or call 973-562-6508.

CHAPTER 19
SUNSET TO SUNRISE

The punishment which the wise suffer who refuse to take part in the government, is to live under the government of worse men.
— PLATO

Policing in our nation is evolving technologically along with the rest of the world. Law enforcement agencies are spending millions of dollars on electronic gadgets designed to deliver services more effectively and efficiently. Faxes, computers, emails, text messaging, and cell phones, continue to become a part of our everyday lifestyle.

Yet, with all this advanced electronic gadgetry, not one wire, not one antenna, not one piece of that equipment which is costing local governments millions in tax dollars could ever replace the human spirit, mind, heart, and soul of police officers working to keep our society safe from crime and terrorism.

Today, in this century, we are beginning to realize that all of us are becoming desensitized to each other's problems. However, we all share the same problems. Family, work, and school for example, affect our quality of life; and our quality of life affects our neighborhoods; and if our quality of life declines, the crime rate will begin to soar and our safety will be in jeopardy.

What all of us must keep in mind is that, perhaps for a moment in time, we need to turn the clock back to the "Andy Griffith" and "Mayberry" days of the 1950s when police officers and the citizens of the community knew each other on a first name basis.

We need to return to the days when a stroll down the street to a neighbor's house, or local police precinct would suffice to learn about crime issues, instead of using text messaging or computer bulletin boards to obtain that information.

We need to return to a time when a telephone call was made to a friend or co-worker before an email was sent.

We need to turn back the clock to a time when people would talk to their police, in their neighborhoods, near their homes, instead of through a website.

In the 19th Century, Sir Robert Peele said, *"The police are the public and the public are the police, the police being only the members of the public that are paid to give full-time attention to the duties which are incumbent on every citizen in the interest of the community welfare and existence."*

We are hard-pressed to fulfill those duties via robots, electronics, and other hardware designed to replace the characteristics of the human spirit, mind, body, and soul.

We are hard-pressed to replace a positive working relationship between the people and the police, with answering machines which require a person to the endless pushing of buttons instead of holding a conversation with a real caring human voice.

We are becoming so isolated from each other because of machines replacing man that police in some cities have already replaced police K-9 units with a robot type instruments designed to detect illegal drugs.

Researchers explain that the instrument picks up vapors in the air, similar to what dogs would pick up. If the vapors detect an odor related to controlled and dangerous substances, the instrument will react accordingly.

The instrument can pick up vapors at levels from microscopic to large quantities, only a few feet away. Cocaine is the drug of choice for this instrument at the present time. Once it is perfected, scientists expect to expand its use to bombs, chemicals, and other illegal substances.

Researchers describe the instrument as the size of a phone book, with two antenna protruding from it. The antennas are the "nostrils" which are designed to "smell" vapors in the air. Law enforcement experts say that K-9 units cost close to $100,000 a year to maintain. This new "robot" would cost over 50% less to maintain.

We are spiraling downhill to a time when all of us are going to forget that it is the human heart which produces compassion and the human spirit which produces encouragement to those who seek protection from crime.

There is no machine in existence which can replace the heart and spirit, nor produce the compassion or encouragement a police officer can.

No machine can look you in the eye like a police officer can, or notice the fear on your face like a police officer can, or sense the anxiety in your voice, like a police officer can.

No machine can pat you on the back, give you a shoulder to weep on, or understand the burden you bear, like a police officer can.

Only a good police officer, with a badge carried over his or her heart, can relate to the human tragedy and the human spirit, via community policing methodologies.

The sun must set on traditional policing methodologies and a new sun must rise and shine upon new ideas to meet new challenges the law enforcement community will be required to meet in this new century.

Community policing is America's last best hope to keep this nation as the land of the free and the home of the brave.

CHAPTER 20
TEST YOUR KNOWLEDGE

The Answer Key can be found at the end of this chapter.

Chapter 1: Leadership

1. What is the most difficult problem law enforcement leaders face with regard to community policing?
2. Who is responsible for a law enforcement agency's leadership failures?
3. What is the end result of instability in the leadership structure?
4. What is meant by "ivory tower" leadership?
5. What is the general feeling among patrol officers with regard to the relationship they have with the police agency they work for?
6. What is meant by "dead weight?"
7. Name one major responsibility of the police sergeant.
8. List four characteristics leaders should demonstrate.
9. Define the view from the "physical eye."
10. Define the view from the "mind's eye."
11. What is MBWA?
12. List five effective methods of communication.
13. List three effective leadership skills.

Chapter 2: Changing Times

1. What is a "five percenter?"
2. Define traditional patrol procedures.
3. Define proactive patrol procedures.
4. What is meant by "generation of entitlement?"
5. What is a negatron?
6. Define "blue wall of silence."

Chapter 3: What Happens Local Goes Global

1. What is meant by What Happens Local Goes Global?

2. What two high profile police actions caused nationwide public outrage against the police in the 1990s?
3. What is the key to prevent a local problem from becoming a "global" problem?
4. Is the way officers dress a method of communication? Yes or No.
5. Name one important component for a successful community policing program.

Chapter 4: Basic Essentials

1. Name one imperative police leaders should integrate into the community policing concept.
2. What should police executives convey to police department personnel when implementing the community policing concept?
3. What is a key ingredient to successful management?
4. What is the overall effect on law enforcement when professional standards are lowered?
5. List five model qualifications for entry into the law enforcement profession.

Chapter 5: Management Methodologies

1. What are MBO and TQM?
2. What can MBO trigger in a police agency?
3. Define Micro-Management.
4. List three pitfalls of Micro-Management.
5. What is meant by bottom to top review?
6. Who is part of the "huddle group"?
7. List four benefits of TQM?
8. What does TQM do for morale?
9. Define L-WAID.
10. Define Corporate Knowledge.

Chapter 6: Implementing Community Policing

1. What is the first step police administrators should take when implementing Neighborhood Watch?
2. What is meant by "police mystique"?
3. What is the benefit of positive police-public dialogue?

4. List six steps in organizing a "Town Hall Meeting."
5. List two don'ts when organizing a "Town Hall Meeting."

Chapter 7: Patrol Operations

1. Define traditional patrol procedures.
2. What is meant by reactive patrol?
3. What is meant by proactive patrol?
4. List eight steps which are recommended to integrate Community Oriented Policing into patrol operations.
5. What is PWT?
6. What is Vertical Patrol?

Chapter 8: Quality of Life Policing

1. Why was Project Unity short-lived?
2. What proved to be a major factor in Project Unity's success?
3. List the five steps used in the problem-solving process of Project Unity.
4. What was the key to success with regard to Project Unity?
5. Develop a mission statement for a local police department community policing project.

Chapter 9: America's Youth and Police

1. What war strained police-youth relations?
2. During July 1968, what political party had its convention in Chicago, Illinois?
3. What did the public backlash against the Chicago Police do to the image of police across the nation in 1968?
4. What mind-set is established by police when they become isolated from the public?
5. What tragic incident occurred in 1973 that caused major public relations problems for the police?

Chapter 10: Citizen Surveys

1. What is the value of a citizen survey?
2. How can the police distribute citizen surveys?

3.   List five questions you can ask on a citizen survey form.
4.   How do you rate police officer performance?
5.   Do State Police organizations conduct citizen surveys?

Chapter 11: Diversity, Tolerance, and Hate Crimes

1.   Define Hate Crime.
2.   Are disabled people covered under the Hate Crime Act?
3.   Can a Hate Crime be committed against property?
4.   Describe Operation AIM.
5.   Can anyone be victimized by a Hate Crime?

Chapter 12: Police Community Partnerships
1.   What is Partner to Parents?
2.   List six JPA programs.
3.   List four police community partner programs.
4.   What is a police/clergy alliance?
5.   What is PSP?

Chapter 13: Victim Oriented Policing

1.   What is the benefit of VOP?
2.   What groups of people are most victimized by crime?
3.   How can VOP help crime victims?
4.   What role does the first responding officer play in the VOP process?

Chapter 14: Intelligence Collection

1.   Knowledge is _____.
2.   Can community policing play a role in the collection of intelligence?
3.   Who are the best intelligence collectors in any community?
4.   What is HLSIB?
5.   What is MACA?
6.   What is HTWG?

Chapter 15: America's Volunteers

1.   What American president supported volunteerism?

2. What is VIPS?
3. How valuable to the police department are volunteer police auxiliaries?
4. What is CERT?

Chapter 16: Police-Media Relations

1. Describe present-day police media relations.
2. What can police do to improve police-media relations?
3. Should police departments establish police media relations bureaus?
4. Anyone can talk to the press.   T   F

Chapter 17: An Abundance of Ideas

1. Why are police officers reluctant to embrace community policing?
2. What are some of the problems the publication "Fresh Perspectives" outlined with regard to community policing?
3. Define Adopt-A-Cop.
4. List five community policing programs which can work in your community.
5. What is the benefit of open community meetings?

Chapter 18: Conflict Resolution

1. Identify a problem or conflict in your community and develop a conflict resolution process to solve the problem/conflict.

Chapter 19: Sunset to Sunrise

1. Develop a list of your closing thoughts about community oriented policing.

Answer Key

Chapter 1:
Leadership
1. Page 1
2. Page 2
3. Page 2
4. Page 3
5. Page 2
6. Page 3
7. Page 4
8. Page 4
9. Page 5
10. Page 5
11. Page 7
12. Page 8
13. Page 9

Chapter 2:
Changing
Times
1. Page 12
2. Page 12
3. Page 11
4. Page 13
5. Page 13
6. Page 12

Chapter 3:
What Happens
Local Goes
Global
1. Page 15
2. Pages 15, 16
3. Page 17
4. Page 17
5. Page 18

Chapter 4:
Basic
Essentials
1. Page 19
2. Page 19
3. Page 19
4. Page 20
5. Page 20

Chapter 5:
Management
Methodologies
1. Pages 23, 24
2. Page 23
3. Page 24
4. Page 24
5. Page 24
6. Page 25
7. Page 25
8. Page 25
9. Page 26
10. Page 26

Chapter 6:
Implementing
Community
Policing
1. Page 27
2. Page 27
3. Page 29
4. Page 29
5. Page 30

Chapter 7:
Patrol
Operations
1. Page 31
2. Page 31
3. Page 31
4. Pages 32, 33
5. Pages 34, 35
6. Page 35

Chapter 8:
Quality of Life
Policing
1. Page 40
2. Page 41
3. Page 42
4. Page 43
5. Pages 43, 44

Chapter 9:
America's
Youth and
Police
1. Pages 51, 52
2. Page 52
3. Page 54
4. Page 54
5. Page 54

Chapter 10:
Citizen Surveys
1. Page 73
2. Page 71
3. Page 71
4. Page 72
5. Page 73

Chapter 11:
Diversity,
Tolerance, and
Hate Crimes
1. Page 75
2. Page 75
3. Page 77
4. Page 79
5. Page 80

Chapter 12:
Police
Community
Partnerships
1. Page 81
2. Page 84
3. Pages 82, 83
4. Page 82
5. Page 82

Chapter 13:
Victim Oriented
Policing
1. Page 88
2. Page 86
3. Page 88
4. Page 88

Chapter 14:
Intelligence
Collection
1. Page 89
2. Pages 92, 93
3. Pages 92, 93
4. Page 90
5. Page 90
6. Page 91

Chapter 15:
America's
Volunteers
1. Page 99
2. Page 101
3. Page 101
4. Page 101

Chapter 16:
Police-Media
Relations
1. Page 106
2. Page 114
3. Page 101
4. Page 108

Chapter 17:
Abundance of
Ideas
1. Page 115
2. Page 116
3. Page 117
4. Pages 116-
   thru 131
5. Page 124

Chapter 18:
Conflict
Resolution
1. Essay

Chapter 19:
Sunset to
Sunrise
1. Essay

Index

OTHER TITLES OF INTEREST
FROM LOOSELEAF LAW PUBLICATIONS, INC.

21ˢᵗ Century Policing
Community Policing: A Guide for Police Officers and Citizens
by Lt. Steven L. Rogers

The Verbal Judo Way of Leadership
Empowering the Thin Blue Line from the Inside Up

ice Professionals

cement

s

eer

- *Understanding*
ion
War on Terror
ene

Law.com